The Joy of Writing a Great Cookbook

The Joy of Writing a Great Cookbook

How to Share Your Passion for Cooking From Idea to Published Book to Marketing It Like a Bestseller

Kimberly Yorio

co-founder of YC MEDIA, and book publicist for Julia Child, Jamie Oliver and Emeril Lagasse

PAGE STREET
PUBLISHING CO.

PAGE STREET
PUBLISHING CO.

First published in 2015 by
Page Street Publishing Co.
27 Congress Street, Suite 103
Salem, MA 01970
www.pagestreetpublishing.com

Distributed by Macmillan; sales in Canada by The Canadian Manda Group; distribution in Canada by The Jaguar Book Group.

18 17 16 15   1 2 3 4 5

ISBN-13: 978-1-62414-060-0
ISBN-10: 1-62414-060-2

Library of Congress Control Number: 2014959975

Cover and book design by Page Street Publishing Co.

Printed and bound in the United States

Page Street is proud to be a member of 1% for the Planet. Members donate one percent of their sales to one or more of the over 1,500 environmental and sustainability charities across the globe who participate in this program.

For Thomas

CONTENTS

Foreword

By Jamie Oliver

I threw my first book party in 2013. I'm not sure why I had never thrown one before, but I had just published my 14th cookbook in the U.K., *Jamie's 15-Minute Meals*, and wanted to celebrate and thank all of the people who had been such an amazing team creating these books with me over the years. We invited everyone who had helped us make the books such a success. From Tom Weldon, my original publisher, to David Loftus, my great mate and brilliant photographer who has worked on all of my books, to the art guys, my food team of recipe testers, my editorial team, and of course my staff and family. Kim Yorio, of course, was one of them, my secret weapon in the U.S. market. But there was one guest who really stood out. Mrs. Murphy, my special education teacher from primary school.

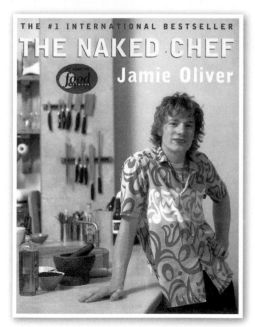

Her arrival was a surprise to me, and I'm not embarrassed to write that we both welled up with tears when we saw each other. For a dyslexic kid who could barely read in primary school to write a book and see the teacher who had helped him all those years ago was really emotional.

No one was more surprised than I was when I published my first cookbook. *The Naked Chef* was a collection of recipes that I had written on scraps of paper, saved in a bin liner and pulled out when the TV people explained we needed a companion book to go with my first television series.

What I wanted to communicate in my cookbooks, even way back then, was that cooking from scratch is fun and easy, and that anyone can do it with the right encouragement and directions. I don't bother with superaccurate measurements (why should you measure olive oil if two glugs into the pan will work just fine?) and try to make the dishes sound appealing and fun. I like the idea of people picking up my books and not being too snooty about food. It's business, there's no mucking about, it's pulling your finger out and saying: "Let's create some bloody good cooking for busy people." In that spirit, I write all my recipes as if I am talking to a mate. I've also made sure that every cookbook I've ever written has been fully illustrated and I've had the honor to work with David Loftus on almost every single one of them. I also have been really lucky that our art director from Penguin, John Hamilton, lets us partner with him to design the books in the way that will make the most sense for the material. That's the key—there are a million ways to write a cookbook, but how you present the material, your photography, your design and your style can make all the difference.

In my book *30-Minute Meals,* I used step-by-step pictures to show people how to make each dish as quickly and efficiently as possible—it's all a bit family and a bit DIY and I love that. It's bold colors, dark meats, light sauces and contrasting salads. When I was coming up with the meals and started tweaking recipes, I was almost cooking by color. Not only would you have textures—something crispy with something soft—but I'd also be putting something dark with something light. I think that is a really beautiful way to cook, and it really worked for that book.

In *15-Minute Meals,* I just liked the simplicity of the dishes, and the finished dish said quite a lot—not just about how cool it looks but also how to serve it, so I did the opposite of *30-Minute Meals* and only took one picture, and stripped the words right back. I want people to cook it quickly and for it to work. People are looking at these pictures saying, "No way, I can't do that in 15 minutes, you're just saying that because you're a chef," but a little read of these stripped down words and they are convinced they can. We have had students cooking them in 15 minutes—we have done all the hard work, all of the screwing up, so you can just get on with it.

I am pretty sure that's exactly what Kimbo is trying to do in this book—all the hard work so you can just get on with writing the book you love and selling it like crazy. Kimbo, Kimberly Yorio as she is known to you, has been my American publicist since I started with *The Naked Chef* in America in 2000. On top of her crazy good palate, relationships with all of the top chefs and incredible Jersey Girl temper, she knows the American market better than anyone I've met. She has guided me through all of the national television shows and magazine interviews, sorted out my messages—no easy feat given that I am promoting different books and shows in different countries on different days. What I respect about Kimbo is that she always tells me the truth. Unlike most publicists who tell you what you want to hear, she presents the good and the bad and always offers a way to make it better. She's been by my side on every book in America and Canada, plus all of my shows, products and for my Foundation. Kimbo knows a thing or two about cookbooks and how to write a good one. Read this book. Take her advice. And just get on with it!

Good luck and Bless,
—Jamie O

Introduction

I had no idea how big the cookbook market was when I started. As a kid, my mother cooked with recipes from women's magazines and The Betty Crocker Recipe Card File. I used to love to flip through those cards trying to narrow down my birthday cake options. One year it was a gingerbread house covered in Necco Wafers and another was a giant white rabbit covered in coconut. (Wilton had just started selling those animal pans and I just had to have one!)

But cookbooks? In addition to the card file, we had maybe two other books—an orange Betty Crocker general cookbook and a *Woman's Day* compendium. We were a Betty-heavy household. So imagine my surprise when, as a young woman early in my career, I found people who were absolutely crazy for cookbooks—and this was before the Food Network.

I've worked with cookbooks for 23 years out of my 25-year career, in-house as a publicist and marketing director and as a for-hire publicist and agent. I've coauthored a cookbook (*Magic in the Kitchen* with photographer Jan Bartelsman) for Artisan Books, sold three cookbooks to three different publishers as an agent and written at least 10 cookbook proposals.

I've worked on the publicity campaigns for close to 1,000 books by many of the finest and biggest names and brands in the food world today, including Julia Child, Emeril Lagasse, Jamie Oliver (the world's bestselling cookbook author today), Rachael Ray, Sheila Lukins, Barbara Kafka, Paul Prudhomme, Lidia Bastianich, Judy Rodgers, Ferran Adrià and The Culinary Institute of America. From James Beard Award winners to IACP award winners to mass-market bestsellers and everyone in between.

Writing a cookbook isn't as easy as jotting down a few recipes and sending it off to a publisher. To get a cookbook deal (or even to self-publish successfully) you need something unique to offer. You should have an established body of work which includes quality recipes, a distinctive point of view and a platform on which to sell your book. If you have all of those things—or are on the path to developing them—this book is for you.

 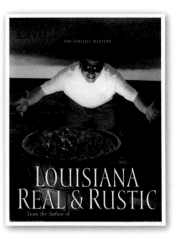 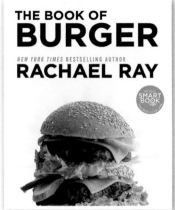 

The Joy of Writing a Great Cookbook will show you how to get from great idea to bookstore shelves (or, at the very least, Amazon). You will learn how to create a compelling proposal, write a good recipe and take a great picture, as well as how to develop a platform, execute a marketing strategy and throw yourself one hell of a book tour.

This book is the culmination of 20-plus years in an industry I love. I have written this book to share the insights and experiences of many of the best people in the industry. Publishers, authors, recipe testers, food stylists, journalists, bloggers, Pinners, celebrity chefs and agents have contributed advice and expertise to help you create a bestselling cookbook, whether you choose the traditional route with an agent and book publisher or strike out on your own and self-publish.

Whether you work your way through this book from the beginning or dip in where you need to, the advice I have gathered will guide you through the process of writing a brilliant cookbook, from forming the initial idea right on through your very first book signing. It's a long and sometimes lonely journey, but—armed with this book—I hope you find not only great advice but support and encouragement.

PART ONE

Selling In

Chapter 1

The Successful Cookbook

⁓

I worked on my first cookbook in 1993 BFN (Before Food Network!) as a senior publicist focused on cookbooks at William Morrow—the most successful cookbook publisher of the time. Morrow had published numerous *New York Times* bestselling authors ranging from PBS star Graham Kerr, *The Galloping Gourmet* and legendary Louisiana chef Paul Prudhomme, to microwave maven Barbara Kafka, syndicated TV cook Mr. Food, esteemed cook Lynne Rossetto Kasper and product hawker extraordinaire, the Juiceman. These cookbooks sold millions of copies *each*.

Cookbooks have traditionally been very good business for publishers. Unlike the latest novel or nonfiction titles, which have limited life spans, cookbooks can stay relevant and marketable for years. Success for a cookbook can be more than financial, too. According to bestselling cookbook author Michael Ruhlman (*Ruhlman's Twenty*, *Charcuterie*) in a blog post on Ruhlman.com (a blog to read regularly if you don't already):

> "As far as I'm concerned, what makes it [a cookbook] successful is the fact that it encourages people to cook. That's my main goal. If I can inspire more people to cook, the book is a success. If it furthers and spreads valuable cooking information it's successful. If it adds something new to the world of food and cooking, then it is successful. Those are my definitions of success. They are not regardless of financial success—to me financial success is an indication that people are buying it and spreading the information, and it gives the publisher the confidence to keep investing in me. But a book that makes a lot of money but neither adds something new nor encourages people to cook is not a success in my book."

About his book *Charcuterie* (W.W. Norton, 2005) he continued:

> "This is a success that I am perhaps most proud of. Brian and I were paid a very small advance for what amounted to two years' work ($50,000, split in half, less 15% for the agent, less, oh, at least 15% for taxes. So that's netting $18,000 spread over two years; authors only get half up front, a quarter on delivery, a quarter on publication, typically). We wrote it because we loved the subject, no other reason.

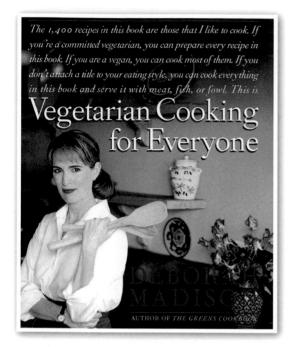

The 1,400 recipes in this book are those that I like to cook. If you're a committed vegetarian, you can prepare every recipe in this book. If you are a vegan, you can cook most of them. If you don't attach a title to your eating style, you can cook everything in this book and serve it with meat, fish, or fowl. This is

Vegetarian Cooking for Everyone

DEBORAH MADISON

AUTHOR OF *THE GREENS COOKBOOK*

"Its success is almost bizarre. It is a book reliant on the two main ingredients that throw fear into most Americans' hearts: animal fat and salt. The recipes don't take 30 minutes, but rather days and even months. If you do them wrong, some of them can kill you.

"The book has sold more than 100,000 copies, and its bacon recipes [have], according to readers and Twitter, changed lives.

"That, to me, is a success more gratifying than any six-figure advance."

When surveying the industry about cookbook success for her blog, Will Write for Food (diannej.com), writer and author of *Will Write for Food* (Da Capo Lifelong Books, 2010) Dianne Jacob received a wide variety of answers. From "earning out my advance" to "positive reviews on Amazon," respondents cited a number of factors. Bestselling author Deborah Madison (*Vegetarian Cooking for Everyone*) offered this:

"You know your book is a success if it accomplished what you wanted it to. It could be different things: selling a lot of copies; getting a lot of print; launching a next step, like a movie; informing and inspiring people; righting a confusion.

"I think of books I've written that have sold a lot and those that have gone out of print or haven't earned back. *Local Flavors,* for example, has never earned out but is, miraculously, still in print. It was a little ahead of its time, but as the interest in farmers' markets has caught up with it, it has really come into play; I'm asked to weigh in on articles on the basis of the book, it's given away at conferences and farmers' markets, so I consider it a success even if by some standards it isn't. *Vegetarian Cooking for Everyone* has been a success financially, but what's most important to me is that it has introduced people to vegetables and other plant foods whether or not they're vegetarian, and when I get e-mails and letters from readers expressing their appreciation for that, I am so gratified. The book did what I hoped it would.

"Another book [*Seasonal Fruit Desserts*] in which I had a mission was in print only for a little over a year. I feel it was a failure even though it was a good book because it didn't get to do what I had hoped, which was to focus on fruit and inspire people to understand and offer ways to enjoy it that were more health supportive than usual. So when you're writing a book and visualizing your audience and thinking about what it is you want the book to say, and if it ends up doing that, it's a success. If it makes a lot of money and gets a lot of print at the same time, that's also a success. But if it doesn't, it's not necessarily a failure.

"The Internet has been a great tool for feedback. Sometimes I feel discouraged about the apparent lack of success of a book, but then I get an e-mail from someone who is a die-hard fan of that book and who really understands it, and that makes it feel like a success."

How do you find the readers who will really understand your book? From the beginning of cookbook publishing in this country, identifying the target market for a book was the key driver for its publication.

A Quick History Lesson

According to the University of Minnesota Media Project, collecting recipes began in early Colonial times, originally passed along by word of mouth and then recorded in collections of handwritten "receipts" (meaning "received rules of cookery"). The first cookbook published in America was a reprint of English bestseller *The Compleat Housewife,* by Eliza Smith, in 1742 by William Parks, a Williamsburg, Virginia printer who believed he had a strong market in Virginia housewives who were interested in the fashions of London.

When *The Compleat Housewife* was published, Ms. Smith described how she altered the cookbook to American "taste," deleting certain recipes, "the ingredients or materials for which are not to be had in this country." Ms. Smith was not only a savvy businesswoman, but seemingly, a feminist, too. In the book's preface, Smith wrote that the male cookbook writers concealed their best recipes from the public and she wanted to write a book that would share all of her secrets. The *Compleat Housewife* title page describes the book as:

"[a] collection of several hundred of the most approved receipts in cookery, pastry, confectionery, preserving, pickles, cakes, creams, jellies, made wines, cordials. Also bills of fare for every month of the year. To which is added, a collection of nearly two hundred family receipts of medicines; viz. drinks, syrups, salves, ointments, and many other things of sovereign and approved efficacy in most distempers, pains, aches, wounds, sores, etc, never before made publick in these parts; fit either for private families or such publick-spirited gentlewomen and would be beneficient to their poor neighbours."

(continued)

  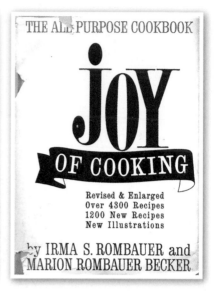

No wonder this book was a bestseller—it included everything a Colonial woman might need. From wines to wounds, Ms. Smith offered an adapted American "receipt" for it. I wish I had been her publicist.

In 1796, 54 years later, the first American published a cookbook, *American Cookery,* by Amelia Simmons. The cookbook publishing industry was established. Close to 160 titles were published in the first half of the 19th century. The early American cookbook was usually divided into three parts, with sections on cooking, medicine and household hints. With little help available to homemakers, these early "receipt" books offered much more than directions for cooking a chicken. These books taught women how to set up and run their households.

By the mid 1800s, organizations devoted exclusively to women's interests started springing up across the country. As a way to spread their teachings (women were offered very little formal education in the 19th century) and values and to raise money, these organizations began publishing compilation recipe books and this tradition continues to this day. The Junior League cookbooks remain bestsellers and even Irma Rombauer's American classic, *The Joy of Cooking*, originally published in 1922, began as a handout for students in a cooking class at the St. Louis First Unitarian Women's Alliance. Around this time, commercial manufacturers began to produce cookbooks as promotional literature for their products. They were given away free for advertising purposes and early titles included *The Magic Baking Powder Cookbook,* published by E.W. Gillett, Co. in 1930-something. It was 9 inches by 6 inches and was 32 pages long.

Bestseller Spotlight: The Joy of Cooking

The Joy of Cooking is almost as famous for its controversies as it is for its extraordinary commercial success. Reading through the various editions is more than a cooking lesson—*The Joy of Cooking* books are a telling of American culinary history. Its revisions track the evolution of American cuisine from 1931 to today. Want to know when Americans began cooking with broccoli or using refrigerators instead of iceboxes? Check the *Joy*.

Written and self-published in 1931 as a way to support her family, by a completely novice cook and St. Louis housewife whose husband had committed suicide, *The Joy of Cooking: A Compilation of Reliable Recipes with a Casual Culinary Chat,* as it was originally titled, has been in print continuously since 1936 and has sold more than 18 million copies.

Ms. Rombauer recruited her daughter, Marion Rombauer Becker, who taught at an art school, to do the cover, interior design and illustrations. Working on weekends from 1930 to 1931, Marion designed the cover, which depicted Saint Martha of Bethany, the patron saint of cooking, slaying a dragon. She also produced silhouette cutouts to illustrate chapter headings. Ms. Rombauer hired a local printer who made labels for Listerine bottles to print the book.

In 1936, an expanded edition of her book was published by the Bobbs-Merrill Company in Indianapolis. Mrs. Rombauer had no agent and did all of the negotiations herself. The resulting contract, in which Bobbs-Merrill was granted the copyright not only for the 1936 edition but also for the original 1931 version, was the beginning of many years of bitter battles between author and publisher.

The 1936 Bobbs-Merrill edition was like no other commercial cookbook of the time. They chose to retain Mrs. Rombauer's folksy style and anecdotes and her unique style of recipe writing. Instead of listing the ingredients for a dish at the top with preparation directions following, the recipes in the 1936 *Joy* unfolded as narratives, with the ingredients indicated as the need for them arose, with each placed in boldface on a new indented line—preserving a conversational tone throughout the recipe, now known as the action method. Bobbs-Merrill also mounted an aggressive sales push and by the end of 1942, the second edition had gone through six printings and sold 52,151 copies.

Her next book in 1939, *Streamlined Cooking*, was a collection of recipes that could be prepared in less than 30 minutes, with an emphasis on the use of canned and frozen foods. Never a commercial success in its own right, many of the book's recipes instead became part of the next edition of *Joy* that was published in 1943. This edition included material aimed at helping readers deal with wartime rationing restrictions. Mrs. Rombauer was always conscious that cooks would have more success if they had a friend in the kitchen. Sales of this edition were phenomenal: From 1943 through 1946, a total of 617,782 copies were sold, surpassing sales of the main competitor, *The Boston Cooking School Cook Book* by Fannie Merritt Farmer.

In 1946, *Joy* was revised again and this sixth edition removed the references to wartime rationing and added in more of the *Streamlined Cooking* recipes. At this point, Mrs. Rombauer was 69 and her health was in decline. Still battling with the publisher, she wanted to ensure that *Joy* remained in the family and negotiated a contract that made her daughter Marion sole successor of any future editions.

Relations between Mrs. Rombauer and Bobbs-Merrill continued to deteriorate and her daughter had to step in. Marion gradually assumed more and more responsibility, at first regarding the book's design, and eventually its content. The 1951 edition was published with Marion Rombauer Becker listed as the coauthor, and she received 40 percent of the royalties.

Marion was a passionate advocate of healthy eating and "her" 1951 edition removed most of the canned and frozen foods from the recipes. She increased the emphasis on whole grains and fresh produce. Throughout this entire time, the Rombauers and Bobbs-Merrill continued to battle in courts. Bobbs-Merrill wanted to add photographs to the books but the Rombauers refused. As a compromise, they added line drawings. Perhaps because of all of the legal tension, the 1951 edition was rife with errors and a corrected edition was issued in 1952 and another with a new index in 1953.

Mrs. Rombauer died in 1962 and Bobbs-Merrill released a new edition without Marion's consent. Marion corrected the book in 1963 and 1964 and arranged for Bobbs-Merrill to exchange copies of the 1962 edition for later corrected ones for any customers who requested them.

The 1964 edition marks the debut of the two-volume mass-market paperback edition that is still widely available in used bookstores. The 1964 edition was also released as a single-volume, comb-ring bound, paperback mass-market edition in November 1973 and distributed into the early 1990s.

The 1975 edition was the last to be edited by Marion and remains the most popular in the marketplace. More than 1,000 pages long, it became a staple in kitchens throughout the country. Though many of the sections may feel dated, the 1975 edition remained in print, primarily in various inexpensive paperback editions, until the "75th Anniversary Edition" was released in 2006.

After the 1975 edition, the *Joy* remained unchanged for close to 20 years. Publisher Simon & Schuster now owned the *Joy* copyright and wanted to relaunch an all-new, totally modern *Joy* in 1993. Under the supervision of Marion's son, Ethan Becker, award-winning and dominating cookbook editor Maria Guarnaschelli, formerly of William Morrow, conceived the 1997 edition and published the Scribner imprint. This edition proved to be hugely controversial as it completely reimagined what *Joy* could be. They used the concise style of Mrs. Rombauer, but dropped the conversational first-person narration. And instead of a dedicated home cook, Guarnaschelli tapped an extraordinary team of esteemed professionals to pen sections of the book. The 1997 version, originally sold with the title *The All-New, All-Purpose Joy of Cooking*, was reissued in February 2008 with the title *The 1997 Joy of Cooking* and is comprehensive, targeted to a modern, sophisticated home cook. The dream team of contributors was listed in the introduction and it included many of the biggest names in the field, including Marion Nestle, who contributed the "Diet, Lifestyle & Health" section, Peter Reinhardt on "Yeast Breads," Dorie Greenspan on "Pancakes, Waffles, French Toast & Doughnuts" and Alice Medrich and Emily Luchetti on "Quick Breads, Pies, Tarts and Cakes." (This is the edition I cook from and this coincided with my entry into the cookbook world. At one point in cookbook circles the only question people had was if "you were working on the *New Joy*." Love her or hate her, Maria Guarnaschelli knew how to create news. The *New Joy,* as we called it, rocketed to the top of the bestseller lists with as many articles written about the behind-the-scenes drama as there were about the actual book.)

To right the perceived sins of the 1997 edition and perhaps more likely to generate another huge wave of sales, Scribner published the 75th Anniversary Edition in 2006. This massive eighth edition includes 4,500 recipes and returned Mrs. Rombauer's original voice to the book. The new/old version returned many simpler recipes and recipes assisted by ready-made products, such as cream of mushroom soup and store-bought wontons, which had been removed in the 1997 edition. The 2006 edition also brought back both the cocktail and frozen desserts sections, and restored much of the information that was deleted in the 1997 edition. They added a new section of "Joy Classics" that contains 35 recipes from 1931 to 1975 as well as a new nutrition section.

Both versions of *The Joy of Cooking* continue to sell to this day and an active web community has been launched by both the Becker and Rombauer families at www.thejoykitchen.com. You can also find them on Facebook, Instagram and Twitter.

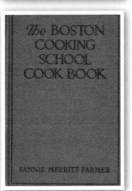

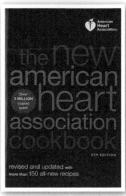

Lists: Bestselling Cookbooks of All Time

According to SeriousRankings.com, "The Top Ten Bestselling Cookbooks of All Time" are:

1. *Betty Crocker's Picture Cook Book* (1950)—65 million

2. *Better Homes and Gardens New Cook Book* (1930)—40 million

3. *Joy of Cooking,* Irma Rombauer (1931)—18 million

4. *The American Woman's Cook Book,* Ruth Berolzheimer (1939)—8 million

5. *In the Kitchen with Rosie: Oprah's Favorite Recipes,* Rosie Daley (1994)—8 million

6. *Crockery Cookery,* Mable Hoffman (1975)—6 million

7. *Fix-It and Forget-It Cookbook: Feasting with Your Slow Cooker,* Dawn J. Ranck and Phyllis Pellman Good (2000)—5 million

8. *The Fannie Farmer Cookbook* (1896)—4 million

9. *Better Homes and Gardens Eat and Stay Slim* (1968)—3.9 million

10. *The New American Heart Association Cookbook* (1973)—3 million

   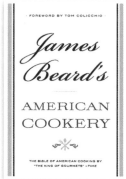 

   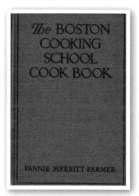 

And *The Village Voice* ranked the "Best Cookbooks of All Time"

1. *The Essentials of Classic Italian Cooking* by Marcella Hazan (Knopf, 1992)

2. *Mastering The Art of French Cooking* by Julia Child, Louisette Bertholle and Simone Beck (Knopf, 1961)

3. *The Joy of Cooking* (Scribner, various editions 1931–2006)

4. *James Beard's American Cookery* by James Beard (Little, Brown and Company, 1980)

5. *Land of Plenty: A Treasury of Authentic Sichuan Cooking* by Fuchsia Dunlop (W.W. Norton, 2003)

6. *One Spice, Two Spice: American Food, Indian Flavors* by Floyd Cardoz with Jane Daniels Lear (William Morrow, 2006)

7. *All About Braising: The Art of Uncomplicated Cooking* by Molly Stevens (W. W. Norton, 2004)

8. *Authentic Mexican: Regional Cooking From the Heart of Mexico* by Rick Bayless (William Morrow, 1987)

9. *The Boston Cooking School Cook Book by Fannie Merritt Farmer* (Originally published in 1896. Gramercy, 1997)

10. *The New Book of Middle Eastern Food* by Claudia Roden (Knopf; Revised edition, 2000)

On Public Relations

J. D. McCLATCHY

NEW AND SELECTED POEMS

A press has written to Knopf objecting to the jacket art on J.D. McClatchy's *Plundered Hearts*.

The printer writes: "I just took a look at the upcoming JD McClatchy book. I knew the cover is based on an artist's photographic work.

Words of Wisdom:
Paul Bogaards, Executive Vice President, Director of Media Relations, Knopf Doubleday

Paul Bogaards is a legend in the publishing industry for his outspoken views, take-no-prisoners attitude and 30-year track record of publishing bestsellers. He has spent years working with the legendary Knopf editors who all share an incredible passion for their authors and books. He wanted to experience that same passion, so now in addition to running the publicity department at Knopf Doubleday, Bogie, as he is called, acquires and edits cookbooks. His bestselling authors include Suzanne Goin, Dr. Andrew Weil, Lidia Bastianich and the Neelys of Food Network fame. Bogie has always been a mentor for me and a bit of an oracle as well, and so I share his words of wisdom on cookbook publishing in Chapter One. For his words of wisdom on everything else, check out his Tumblr at http://paulbogaards.tumblr.com/.

➼ The first book I was assigned to publicize was *The Way to Cook* by Julia Child. Working with Julia was an eye-opening experience. She surprised me almost every day with how smart she was about the business of her books. She was very down-to-earth and knew how to connect with her readers. Perhaps most importantly, she was a great teacher. When you read her work, you became a better cook because the knowledge transfer was so thorough. Many authors go straight to the recipe and forget about the teaching. Julia made no assumptions about people in the kitchen. She assumed that people didn't know a lot and wanted to show her readers that cooking wasn't complicated if you followed the directions. She was very clear on the right way to do things and it came through in all of her books.

➼ The first cookbook I acquired was *Sunday Suppers at Lucques*, Suzanne Goin's first book. Suzanne was an esteemed chef but not hugely famous. She had one restaurant in Los Angeles, was opening a second but wasn't on television or featured very prominently in the press. But her proposal had an incredible clarity of vision. I had the great good fortune to work with Judith Jones (legendary editor of Julia Child and Marcella Hazan, among others) for more than 24 years before she retired. One of the first things she said to me was, "Always be attentive to the voice. The voice of the writer has to animate the page."

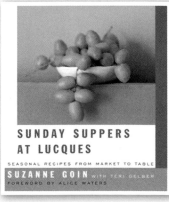

(continued)

➾ Conceptually, Suzanne's book was unique—sharing meals over the course of many Sundays family-style and broken out seasonally. Suzanne was a protégé of Alice Waters and a practitioner of farm-to-table cuisine, a proponent of using the best, locally-sourced ingredients. The recipes sounded wonderful and it all came through in the proposal. I took the recipes home to test and they tested really well. She was very thorough and in every recipe came a lot of detail. The attention, rigor and discipline that she gained working as a chef transferred to the page. Those qualities are what sold me—not so much her successful restaurant, but what she had put on the page.

➾ A revolution of sorts is happening in the United States and around the world. People are more attentive than ever to all things culinary. They have better access to produce, meat and seafood. As consumers become more educated about their palates and food they become savvier about what makes a successful cookbook. And you'll see it borne out in the marketplace. I wouldn't call Suzanne Goin's or Thomas Keller's books simple, but there is a robust market for that kind of detail.

➾ A good cookbook has to be well written and the author has to have a point of view. A good cookbook author tells a story, gives a narrative framework and a great deal of connective tissue that drives together all of the material from the introduction to the chapter openings, to the headers and most importantly the recipe directions themselves.

➾ Too many books fall into what I call the "Chop, Mix, Stir" category. Chop. Mix. Stir. Dish. A cookbook author has to have the ability to recognize what determines the outcome of a successful dish. It's not chop, mix stir. It's taste, smell, temperature, texture, ingredients. It's all of those things.

➾ Make sure the recipes work. So many books are published where that is not the case. It's kind of crazy—inexcusable really.

➾ In our changing world, we've lost the ability to broadcast, and gained the ability to narrowcast. Find a niche that is uniquely your own—Southern baking, canning, pickling. There are all kinds of narrows out there, in there. Pick one.

➾ If you're serious about writing a cookbook and get down to the moment where you're writing a proposal, be familiar about other books in your category and answer these questions: Who are you? Why does your food matter? Why does the world need your book?

Not all great cookbooks are bestsellers. I have worked on many brilliant books that don't create traction in the marketplace. And sadly a great number of mediocre books achieve extraordinary commercial success because of the profile of the author. This author hopes you will strive for greatness in your work, but in the meantime, we will get to work on building your platform.

Chapter 2

Build Your Platform

Selling your first cookbook won't be easy. Chances are you'll have worked for years in the food industry before you get your big break. The cookbook business becomes more competitive each day with publishers desperately reading the tea leaves to try and figure out where to place their bets, whether big or little. Kids are graduating from culinary school and looking for jobs as celebrity chefs. No one wants to be a cook anymore—oh no, people want to be stars. And stars get big book deals. Well, very many stars have to align for all those dreams to come true, so let's focus on what you can do, and that's building a platform.

The term platform came in vogue in the early 2000s—and what it refers to is a marketing platform. In *Writer's Digest*, Christina Katz describes it this way: "Platform is a simple word to describe a complicated process—a process that's been shrouded in mystery until recently. If you're wondering what the difference is between a completely unknown writer and a well-known writer, I can tell you. The well-known writer has influence. In order for you to build influence, you need to create and launch a platform that communicates your expertise, credibility and integrity to others quickly and concisely."

To start developing your platform, you'll need to make some important choices about your topic, audience and the ways you interact best with them. I have identified the five critical planks you need to build a solid platform.

Five Critical Planks in Your Platform

1. A Clearly Defined Brand
2. A Unique Selling Proposition
3. Visibility in Your Industry
4. A Social Media Presence
5. Traditional Media Experience

1. A CLEARLY DEFINED BRAND

Who are you? What do you do? Why will anyone care? The answer could be as simple as, "I am a vegan baker," but that's only the beginning of the story. How are your vegan baked goods *more* special than the next guy's? I choose that poor grammar with intent. It's not simply enough to be special in this climate. You have to be more special. In fact, you have to be the most special.

Erin McKenna, founder of the now-very-famous Babycakes brand, was a girl in the fashion industry who was allergic to wheat and dairy and a homebody in a very glamorous business. She told *TheAwl.com*, "I wanted to open a place I'd like to go to. I've never been a big partier—going to a bakery after dinner was my kind of club and in New York, there are so many incredible specialty bakeries. I felt left out. So I figured I'd just open a place that I'd be stoked to find." Her bakery was unique not just in the vegan goods offered, but in how she offered them. She continued, "I really wasn't setting out to be a baking goddess or whatnot. I just wanted to open a fun place and make some good food, share it, listen to the music I like, dress girls up in uniforms, eat cookies all day." Soon after opening, the bakery earned great reviews and a celebrity following. Erin started a blog, opened a second location in Los Angeles (eventually a third in Downtown Disney in Orlando), published her first bestselling cookbook in 2009 and her second bestseller in 2011. Babycakes is 100 percent Erin's vision and any consumer would know exactly what it is by visiting her stores, reading her blog or baking from her cookbooks.

2. A UNIQUE SELLING PROPOSITION

Why did Erin McKenna's "fun place" become such a huge success? Was it because the products were so delicious? Or because all the girls who work in the bakery are cute and wear killer uniforms? Or because it filled a need in the marketplace? Or because Erin has a unique and consistent voice? Of course the answer is all of the above. According to Wikipedia, "a unique selling proposition (USP) is a marketing concept first proposed as a theory to explain a pattern in successful advertising campaigns of the early 1940s. The USP states that such campaigns made unique propositions to the customer that convinced them to switch brands. The term has been used to describe one's 'personal brand' in the marketplace. Today, the term is used in other fields or just casually to refer to any aspect of an object that differentiates it from similar objects."

You are no longer just a great cook or baker or blogger (and I am assuming if you are ready to write a book, then you have achieved a level of greatness in your craft), you are now a brand, and to make a great brand you must have a clear USP. How do you differentiate yourself from the thousands of cookbook authors and cooks out there? It starts with research and soul-searching.

Put yourself in your reader's or publisher's shoes and ask yourself the hard questions. Why are your recipes the ones to choose? How are they different or special? Are they shorter? Longer? More specific? For a type of cuisine that has never been covered? Solve a need in the marketplace, i.e, fast gluten-free? Think about Erin's bakery—nothing existed like it before. So if you're a vegan baker, how will your offer be better or different? What will your focus be?

Consider what motivates your readers' behavior and buying decisions. In whatever field you've been working in, you have had experience with customers. What have your customers enjoyed the most from you? What do they ask for? When Erin started, she was her own market research. She knew there was no fun place to get vegan baked goods in New York City, which is why she had been baking at home and perfecting her own recipes. She also knew there were thousands of girls just like her who would love a great vegan cupcake or cookie. Putting together the demand with a great product created her huge success.

Uncover the real reasons readers want your recipes instead of a competitor's. Why you? Why now? And really, how do you know? The most exciting part of a successful blog is the immediate reaction you get after posting a recipe. Within minutes, you can tell if people like a recipe and want to make it from their comments. Think like a business and your blog or even a dish in your restaurant is more than just a post or a plate, but an opportunity for market research that will help you refine your offer and create your USP.

3. VISIBILITY IN YOUR INDUSTRY

To get a cookbook published in this competitive marketplace, your work and/or personality need to stand out. Pam Krauss, publisher of Pam Krauss Books (and longtime editor of Ina Garten and Giada DeLaurentiis, to name-drop just two of the hundreds of bestselling, high-profile cookbook authors she has edited and published over the years), has never bought an unsolicited manuscript. She explained, "On some level a prospective author needs to know someone—whether a journalist or a chef colleague or even a friend of a photographer. If we receive the rare unagented submission, it is because they were referred by someone we know." She continued, "Anybody interested in writing a cookbook proposal is already in the food world. The likelihood that uncovering grandma's recipe box is a golden ticket is almost zero. Our submissions come from professionals who are chefs, or bloggers, own a small shop in Brooklyn, run a stall at Smorgasburg, or even lately, someone with a massive Pinterest following." To get a cookbook published you have to be actively in the business in some way creating a name for yourself and building a network of professionals who will offer you their support.

Gaining visibility begins with networking. Resist the urge to scream. I hate networking too because it feels so transactional and mercenary: I want to meet this person so they can help me. That is not only a horrible motivation, but doomed to fail. Flip the script. The only way to build a solid and supportive network is to focus on what you have to offer others—not what they have to offer you.

4. A SOCIAL MEDIA PRESENCE

Just two years ago, Facebook was for stalking ex-boyfriends and people from high school. Now it's a major tool for marketers—and the easiest way to create awareness and engagement with your brand. Chapter 8 is dedicated to social media, so head there for the immersion. It's important to note here that a social media presence is no longer optional. If you don't have an online community—even a very small one—a publisher won't take you seriously. The only thing a great social media presence requires to develop is time—and boy does it take a lot of time. Post regularly and engage. This is not a one-way channel. Social media is about interaction. You'd better start interacting.

5. TRADITIONAL MEDIA EXPERIENCE

Not as easy to develop as a social media platform, but just as important, some experience with traditional media is a necessary component of your platform. Whether you have been featured or contribute to magazines or newspapers or blogs, or appear on television, you need some outside third-party validation of your work. Appearances on shows or in blogs demonstrate a demand for your offerings, not just from those with whom you actively engage on social media channels.

Spotlight:
Bestselling Cookbook Author Archetypes

➽ Bloggers
➽ Celebrities: A, B, C and otherwise
➽ Food Television Personalities
➽ Journalists and/or Food Writers
➽ National Brands
➽ Niche or Not-So-Niche Dietary Focus
➽ Restaurant Chefs

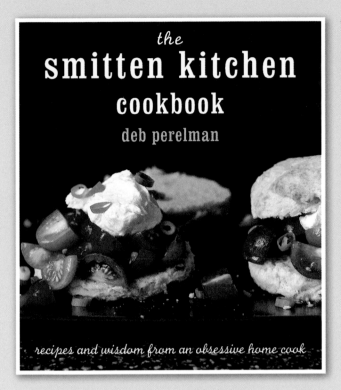

the
smitten kitchen
cookbook
deb perelman

recipes and wisdom from an obsessive home cook

Words of Wisdom:
Smitten Kitchen

Deb Perelman of the Smitten Kitchen blog is a home cook, mom, photographer and celebrated food blogger. And she loves to cook. She isn't a chef or a restaurant owner—she's never even waitressed. Cooking in her tiny Manhattan kitchen was, at least at first, for special occasions—and, too often, an unnecessarily daunting venture. Deb found herself overwhelmed by the number of recipes available to her. Deb is a firm believer that there are no bad cooks, just bad recipes. She has dedicated herself to finding the best of the best and adapting them for the everyday cook—the ones with little time to spare, little money to burn on unpronounceable ingredients and little help in the kitchen. After much prodding, she wrote and photographed her first cookbook in 2012, *"The Smitten Kitchen Cookbook,"* which spent 10 weeks on *The New York Times* Best Seller list. Deb is as generous with her time as she is with her recipes. In this Q&A she shares her debut cookbook experience.

How was your approach to writing your cookbook different from working on the blog every day?

It wasn't hugely different. I was trying to keep the process the same—write a story and a recipe and illustrate with a few pictures. I was very comfortable with the process because at the time I was writing the book I had been doing the site for four to five years. In actuality there was a whole different level of stressors to writing the book. The site is just me—with the cookbook there were publishers, editors, art directors. And, of course, when something goes to print you really can't change it, which created a much higher stress and worry level.

I would guess that one of the greatest things about blogging is your autonomy and total control over your finished product. What was it like working with a publishing team who had opinions and input and authority over your work?

I had certainly heard all the horror stories from other blogger friends about books that they had done and their publishers didn't understand their voice or their style and I was really worried about all of this going in. But my experience was nothing like that. Everyone knew what they had bought with me and where I was coming from. I never felt like anyone was stomping on my creative style. Don't get me wrong, it was a huge surprise to get those first manuscript edits. So much red pen—it looked like a bloodbath. I swear

(continued)

it looked like someone had spilled cranberry juice on the page. The copy editor was amazing and a total surprise. I was forever impressed with her ability to check the consistency. I would get notes, "on page 52 you call for oz. and on 97 ounces. Which would you prefer?"

❧ Very few cookbook authors actually photograph and style their books themselves. What was that process like?

I would guess that's because most cookbook authors aren't insane. I always said I wouldn't do the photos. I didn't want my book to be lined up on the shelf next to all of the professionally done photographs and appear lacking. But the truth is that when it was conceived what *The Smitten Kitchen Cookbook* would look like, it would always look like the blog. And for that to happen, I had to photograph it.

I don't have fancy plates, professional lighting, food stylist skills or a food stylist hanging around. I tried to remember that I am actually presenting food the way it looks—the way it will look if you make the recipe. So often when you take a recipe from a magazine the photo looks absolutely gorgeous and then when you cook it at home, it just doesn't live up. I wanted people to be able to feel excited about what they cook and that their food matches the photos, too.

❧ In every post and in the book, I really feel like you're considering everyone else. It doesn't feel like this all about you.

Whenever you're on a blog with comments and interaction it's very clear that it's not about your story. It's always been a conversation. At this point on Smitten Kitchen there are 200 people talking about something and I am only one of them. I want to be a good conversationalist among my readers and I think those skills are very important. Because I think my writing style developed through having blogs and I am speaking to people every day, it's very hard to write as if I am the most important person in the room. I am the host of the conversation.

Lemon Squares, *The Smitten Kitchen Cookbook*

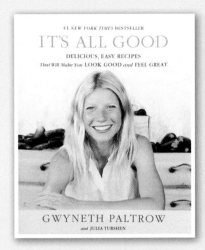

Words of Wisdom:
Matthew Ballast, Vice President, Director of Publicity, Grand Central Publishing

Matthew Ballast has been working with bestselling authors for the past 15 years. He has recently taken on cookbooks and had the good fortune to publish bestsellers, including books written by Gwyneth Paltrow and Rocco DiSpirito. But it's not just big stars that grace his list and the bestseller list. One of his current favorites is the *Four and Twenty Blackbirds* cookbook, written by two sisters from a bakery in Brooklyn. Matthew has seen it all in this business and for his contribution, I asked him to share a top five. He chose five things a first-time author could do to help his or her cause.

Top Five Things First-Time Authors Can Do That will Actually Help Their Cause—aka How to Build a Profile

➡ **Create a strong social media presence.** It can begin with your blog—so many cookbook authors now started from their blog—but it's not limited to a blog. Make sure you are tying everything together—your brand or personal website, your Facebook page, Twitter, Instagram and Pinterest accounts, your Tumblr, YouTube channel, whatever presence you have online all tied together. Don't forget it's a numbers game. If you can get into the thousands of fans and followers, that is the ideal goal, but we also look for trends and interaction. Are you increasing followers and fans? By how much? Which posts are yielding the most engagement? How engaged are you with your fan base? It's not enough to just throw something up. You need to be constantly interacting with and cultivating your community. We need to know that when we publish your book, your fans will be there ready to buy. And to that end, when your book is published, make sure you have direct links to sell like bn.com or Amazon.

(continued)

I like Facebook for cookbook authors, but Pinterest seems to be a growing platform. Anything photo driven is preferred—Instagram linking to Facebook is an easy way to show the world what you are cooking and doing. Most authors focus on the social media channel that is most in line with their personality. If you can do short-form chat (chefs LOVE Twitter) then go for it. Just pick one, be present, link them wherever possible and keep it up.

▷ **Get TV Experience**. Even if you're just going on your local morning news show or doing brief, self-produced videos and posting them on your blog, getting experience in front of the camera is really key—particularly if you don't have a national media platform. We're publishing a book called *Four and Twenty Blackbirds*, a gorgeous book based on a Brooklyn pie shop. The authors, two sisters from South Dakota, had never done TV, but we were able to get them to do a really cute video and then we sent pies to all of the morning shows. The combination of the pies, the video and a Thanksgiving hook got us a "Good Morning America" booking—an amazing get in this competitive climate. Another success story for us was for an adorable book called *Betty Goes Vegan*, a takeoff on Betty Crocker becoming a vegan from a cute Brooklyn couple. They did a great demo video that they posted on their site and that, combined with the great title and subject, got us a booking on "The Today Show." Great video helps at all stages—even in the acquisition process. If an author's package includes great links to video they have a better chance of getting a book deal from us.

▷ **Include Great Food Photography** that you have rights to give to the media. This isn't always as obvious as it should be: Make your dishes look as appealing as possible. Great photos help sales. Make sure your photographs create a sense of your aesthetic style and differentiate you from the other people who are out there, which brings me to my next point.

☞ **Be Unique and Different.** Easier said than done we all know, but it's so important to know how to differentiate your brand from the pack. The sisters from *Four and Twenty* had a story—sisters from South Dakota baking their grandmother's traditional recipes in season and in a way that they hadn't seen in other New York bakeries—and a successful bakery. They are just two sisters baking pies. They had a great track record behind them, almost 3,000 fans on Facebook, 2,000-plus followers on Twitter and an active Instagram account. These girls rose above the pack.

☞ **Know Your Competition, Be Familiar With the Media and Establish a Network.** I know this brings me over my limit, but this is all really important stuff. Before you even think about selling a cookbook, you need to know which other books are out there that are in your category. Too many people think they have no competition. That's nonsense. Thousands of cookbooks are published a year—of course there is competition. You just need to learn how to differentiate yourself from the pack. Get to know the media. Offer to contribute to other blogs or magazines—get out there as much as possible. It's been really helpful when authors have an established network of other cookbook authors or chefs who can give them blurbs for their book or tweet about their book to their friends. The marketplace is changing. I have been happy and surprised to see that cookbook success is happening for more than just Food Network stars and celebrities.

With the rise of social media, building your platform and consequently nurturing your community will become an ongoing and daily ritual. Your supporters and fans want to hear from you and you will want to engage with them as they can become your trusted advisors as you define the focus of your cookbook—the next step on your journey to becoming a published author.

Chapter 3

Get Focused

❦

Oh dear reader, the time has come for the hard work. Chapter One has shown you how difficult this road you've chosen will be and has armed you with examples of success and words of wisdom for your journey. Chapter Two has given you the tools to create a platform—how to create a brand for yourself and showcase your talents to the world. You should by now have a widely read blog, an engaged Facebook community, a plethora of Pinners, a critically acclaimed and hugely profitable restaurant, a wildly successful YouTube channel, a column in a magazine or newspaper, a weekly segment on the local news, a big win on a cooking competition show, a wholly unique style and point of view in the kitchen, plus of course a burning passion to write a book. And the time needed to write, test, photograph, rewrite, retest and rephotograph a cookbook. For we are not just embarking on any old cookbook—we want you to write a great cookbook, and a great cookbook that will sell many copies for years to come. Sound challenging? It is.

What is your cookbook going to be about? How is it going to be different from the thousands of other cookbooks that have already been published? What will make it special? What makes you special? How are you going to communicate all of that specialness? Will your book be chock-full of pictures? Is your recipe style unique? Are your recipes going to be limited to one page and 10 ingredients? What is this cookbook going to teach people? Why will they care? Why will they not just want it, but NEED it in their lives?

Phew. I am overwhelmed just thinking about all of this, so let's break it down and start from the beginning.

The great challenge in writing a great cookbook is that a great cookbook needs to be more than just a collection of great recipes. *Although it also needs to be a collection of great recipes.* A great cookbook is a focused collection of the best, most relevant recipes in your repertoire devoted to a particularly unique subject that you are best suited to author.

Will Schwalbe, a publisher, cookbook editor and founder of Cookstr.com, a website devoted to culling the best recipes from cookbooks, swears that a cookbook will only be successful if you are willing to "kill your darlings." Schwalbe said, "If I am working with an author who is pitching me 100 low-cholesterol treats, but insists on including five high-cholesterol dishes because they are the all-time favorites in his repertoire, I tell him no. And explain that you need a bit of unsentimentality about the work because it's not for you; it's for your reader. Besides, testing recipes that don't belong in the book in the first place will exhaust you, your budget and everyone around you."

Words of Wisdom

T. Susan Chang, the cookbook reviewer for NPR, *The Boston Globe*, and EatYourBooks.com and blogger at *Cookbooks for Dinner* (http://tsusanchang.wordpress.com/) is a woman who knows a thing or two about cookbooks. She's reviewed thousands and is literally testing recipes from books every single day of her life. She wrote a piece for *Publishers Weekly* in 2009 called "10 Things Every Cookbook Publisher Should Know." I'm sharing her "Five Things that Make a Good Cookbook Great." What was true then is true now.

Five Things That Make a Good Cookbook Great

Design plays a role in making a great cookbook, but for the most part, it's the content that separates the wheat from the chaff. The author of a great cookbook has passion to spare, and a vast fund of knowledge. That shows up in the details, whether they're technical, historical, scientific or anecdotal.

1. Great headnotes. Headnotes are what make me fall in love with a cookbook, because that's where the author tells us what this recipe is doing in this book, and why they love it so. It's a place for stories and helpful tips ("if you can't find banana chiles, serranos will do"). Headnotes aren't just decorative—they can give you vital clues. If the author describes how she first was captivated by this recipe because of the smell of perfectly caramelized onions wafting out a window, that gives you a sense of something to watch for in the cooking.

2. "Instant classics." It's always disappointing to buy a cookbook and then find it's filled with recipes for things you already know how to make because they're commonplace: meat loaf, spaghetti carbonara, roast chicken, or a scarcely altered variation on those themes. I always look for instant classics—recipes that aren't overly familiar but are good enough and straightforward enough to adapt as a household standard. *Two Dudes, One Pan*'s baked penne frittata and Dorie Greenspan's chicken tagine with dried apricots are two examples.

3. "What to Look For." This is perhaps the clearest indicator of a great cook and, more importantly, a great teacher. The halfhearted cookbook author might merely say, "Fry for five minutes over high heat," maybe adding a perfunctory "until golden." But gas and electric burners are variable, and times vary. Tell us how the spices should smell when they're toasted, how big the bubbles in the sauce should be when it's simmering properly, how salty the curry paste should be. There's nothing wrong with a wordy recipe—it just shows someone cares.

4. Sidebars, glossaries, indexes. Although we don't use them while we're actually cooking, these peripheral materials distinguish the cookbook that stays on your shelf for years from the one you give away after a season. It's not just the useful information, like how to shop for Japanese groceries, or the equipment you need to make your own pasta. It's the quotes from other cooks, the story about Nana and the fishmonger, the lore that makes your cookbook different from anyone else's.

5. Art. Good design is essential; good art can make a buyer fall in love with your cookbook right there in the store. But don't let your food stylist go so crazy with the shot that it no longer bears a relationship to what the home cook can reasonably produce. Nothing's more infuriating than seeing perfect grill marks on a piece of meat when you've been told to run it under a broiler, or having beautiful little heirloom cherry tomatoes not mentioned in the recipe prettying up a beige risotto under false pretenses. Honest photographs, preferably facing the recipe page, are great. Drawings, whether whimsical or realistic, can work, too. (And type can be every bit as powerful as art. I am partial to the mixed-typeface designs you see more and more of these days—they punch up a page and often help me parse a recipe at speed.)

Of course, these are just my opinions. To some extent, they're arbitrary—yet I've heard cooks here, there and everywhere echo these thoughts. Of course, the single most common refrain you hear among cooks is "I already have too many cookbooks!" But superior content, captivating design and thoughtful editing will overcome that lament every time.

Ask Yourself

To get the most focused content, start with the big questions, and then go deeper and deeper down until you're 100 percent confident that every idea, recipe and bit of ancillary material supports the premise of the book.

1. **Who are you writing this book for?** Think about your target market. Who are they? How many of them exist? What do they want? What do they lack? Are they new cooks? Advanced cooks? Men? Women? Short on time? Hobbyists who want to spend time in the kitchen? Working moms? Stay-at-home moms? You need to build a picture of your reader in your mind and make sure that every recipe is written for this reader.

2. **What do they want from you?** You are not writing this book for yourself. You are writing this book to fill a niche in the marketplace, to teach, to entertain and to add to the culinary education of your market. Make a list of your readers' needs and post it on your wall. Examples might include: technique-driven, under 15 minutes, under 400 calories per serving, gluten-free, uses chicken, butter cakes. Make sure you have five or so defining needs and then constantly check your content against them.

3. **How are your recipes different from the zillions of other recipes that have gone before? Or the hundreds that you have already posted on your blog?** Think about your specific recipe style. How are you going to describe your ingredients? What weights and measures are you going to use? Are you "talking" your reader through the recipe or being more prescriptive? Your writing style could become your unique point of difference in the marketplace, so you need to make sure you stay true to your choice. If you're a blogger, keep in mind that readers won't buy what they can already get free. You want to provide original recipes and perhaps even a completely new direction for your community. If you're a vegan blogger who mostly posts main dishes, maybe a book of vegan desserts should be your first offer. Use your community when testing out concept ideas. Ask them what they want to see in a book from you. That's always a good place to start.

4. **What kind of illustration best supports your content?** Consumers want photographs in their cookbooks. How are you going to use photographs and illustrations to make your book special? The art should never be an afterthought—how you use art can be the differences between a dud and a bestseller. Devise a plan and stick to it. Do you want to incorporate step-by-step pictures or just finished dishes? Will you be styling the pictures yourself or hiring a professional?

5. **What else needs to be in the book?** Your book will include more than recipes. What other material needs to be included? Explanations of ingredients? Highlights of regularly used techniques? Menus? Interviews with other experts?

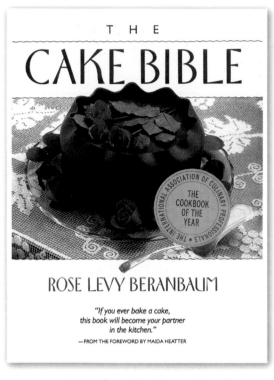

T H E

CAKE BIBLE

THE INTERNATIONAL ASSOCIATION OF CULINARY PROFESSIONALS • THE COOKBOOK OF THE YEAR

ROSE LEVY BERANBAUM

"If you ever bake a cake, this book will become your partner in the kitchen."
—FROM THE FOREWORD BY MAIDA HEATTER

Your cookbook idea should be unique to you. As a matter of fact, you should be the *only* person in the world who could write the book well. Of course that's a high bar, but if you can come close, then you're sure to be successful. You want to write a cookbook about American comfort food with a Southern accent, because you grew up in Virginia, have been blogging for the last five years while showcasing your culinary talents in pop-up restaurants all over the Southeast, and are now ready to take your message and style to the rest of the country? You are the expert and through your expert lens you must now evaluate the relevance of every piece of content in the book.

Consider the context of how you want the work to be received. Should your readers be able to take the book off the shelf in the bookstore and straight into the kitchen? Are you trying to take your readers on more of a journey? What do they need to know about you and the book before they start cooking? In the bestselling cookbook, *The Cake Bible* (William Morrow, 1998), Rose Levy Beranbaum was explicit in her directions in the front matter that if you didn't weigh your ingredients, you wouldn't be able to re-create her results. She was also explicit in her instruction that temperatures of the individual ingredients were also critical to a good result. She was working within the context of creating the most perfect baking cookbook ever written, and to be successful as a reader and baker, you had to follow her directions to the letter. The book was initially published in 1988 to enormous critical acclaim and hit *The New York Times* bestseller list. If you look at the reader reviews on Amazon now, all of the complaints have to do with the rigor to which Rose expects you to follow the recipes. Great results are indeed difficult because she's asking for total immersion in her subject. As a reader, if you don't know the context of the book, there's a chance you will be disappointed. As an author, as long as you provide the context, you have done your job.

You also want to consider the context of the marketplace. For example, Paleo cookbooks are very big right now. A search for "Paleo cookbooks" yields 3,904 results. If you are a Paleo chef and want to publish a book, how are you going to differentiate your content in a saturated marketplace? Given that a cookbook usually takes at least two years from signing the deal to publication, inventing the "next Paleo" may be the blockbuster idea.

> "I am looking for recipes that inspire people and make people talk about them. I want the focus to be on recipes that are usable and also different—recipes that are truly exciting. Good content inspires sales."
>
> —Will Kiester, the Publisher and Editor of Page Street Publishing

Good content inspires sales. What makes good content? There is so much content out there, how do you focus on what's right for a book versus a blog or versus a magazine article? Originality is critical. When Deb Perelman was writing her cookbook, for her, the most important thing was that her recipes were all original and hadn't appeared in the blog. Of course she used the most popular recipes in the blog to guide her recipe list, but for her book, she developed an entirely original collection. She wanted to give her community value for the money they were willing to spend on her and her first cookbook. For her there was no value in simply republishing recipes that had already appeared on her blog. She believed her community expected more from her. Her book hit the bestseller list in the first week.

Publisher Will Kiester tells his authors, "If you've just rattled ten recipes off the top of your head, there's a good chance that your neighbor could do the same thing. Recipes shouldn't be obvious—even if the subject is." Let's take the example of America's favorite comfort food dish, macaroni and cheese. For many, the blue and white box is the gold standard and no recipe would ever be needed. And yet, a search on Google yields more than 4.45 million results—many of which are recipes—and at least nine entire macaroni and cheese cookbooks are selling on amazon.com. So by this standard, should you discard your Mac and Cheese recipe—or the entire idea of a Mac-n-Cheese cookbook out of hand? Not before you go deeper and analyze the variables. What makes a great macaroni and cheese? Is it the texture? Flavor? The shape of the noodle? The PEA (phenylethylamine—an organic compound found in cheese and chocolate that has been shown to release the same hormones that are released during sexual intercourse)? The type of cheese? All of the above? None of the above? Sweet Chick Restaurant in Manhattan and Brooklyn, NY makes their macaroni and cheese with oversized shells, a silky combination of Colby and Cheddar cheeses melted into a Bechamel and then piles it into a round ceramic bowl, tops it with crushed Ritz crackers and butter and broils it in the oven. Worthy of inclusion in a book? Definitely—it's delicious, unique in texture, style, combination of cheeses and even the topping.

In a blog post (and later in her *The Pioneer Woman Cooks!* cookbook,) the famous Pioneer Woman, and first blogger-to-cookbook-author bestselling phenomenon, Ree Drummond, waxes positively rhapsodic about her macaroni and cheese, and in a way that is signature Ree:

There's nothing that can be said.
But there is much to be eaten.
Come, my child...come. I shall take you by the hand and take you where you need to go.
I shall show you the food that is solely responsible for my bones and tissues multiplying and growing at a young age.
It's macaroni and cheese. And it's the only food I consumed until I was about fourteen years old.
Come...come, my child.
I shall show you the way.

So does her recipe live up to our test of what makes a great recipe? She starts with elbow macaroni, which she recommends to buy in bulk because it's cheap, and then adds salted butter, dry mustard for "tangy sharpness," an egg, whole milk, "and cheese. One glorious, beautiful pound of freshly grated cheese. I'm using all sharp cheddar today, but I almost always mix cheeses: Colby, Monterey Jack, Fontina, Mild Cheddar, Pepper Jack...even a little Gruyere if I allow myself to be in denial about how expensive it is."

Ree's recipes (on her blog and in her books) tell stories. They offer a unique perspective, not only in the ingredient choices and method, but in voice—how her instructions play out on the page. She writes about cost, variations and generally reels you in so that you finish reading and want to run into the kitchen to try out her recipe. And that is a great recipe. It delivers originality, context and a unique culinary sensibility. Through her years in writing the blog, Ree, much like Deb Perelman, has created a signature voice that by its nature focuses her concept. Ree executes masterfully what Will Kiester needs to see in a recipe: "It fires on many cylinders and doesn't just work, each recipe gives the reader many things to talk about."

Words of Wisdom:
Will Schwalbe, Cookbook Editor and Founder of Cookstr.com

Will Schwalbe has held many roles in publishing: publisher, editor in chief, cookbook editor, founder of Cookstr.com and author. I've known him since my first day on the job at William Morrow and he has been a tireless source of knowledge, inspiration and now business development, as many of his projects become part of the YC Media family. It was Will who discovered Jamie Oliver at the Frankfurt Book Fair in 1998—before he had been published in the U.K. He has an incredible eye for culinary talent and his author list over the years reads like a "Top of the Pops", including Jamie Oliver, Mollie Katzen, Nigella Lawson, Art Smith, Rocco DiSpirito, the Juiceman and Mr. Food.

He's taught me more than I could possibly ever share in this passage, but as he is the ultimate words guy, I wanted to share his words of wisdom on focusing your content:

➡ The standard line in publishing is that what you want in a book is exactly like last year's bestseller and totally like nothing written ever before. You need to ask yourself: What qualities does this book share with books that have done very well? And what distinguishes it from others? What is your unique culinary perspective? To get to the right answers, you have to start with the right questions, and the right set of beliefs.

▶ Do market research. Go online. Go to local bookstores. Ask friends what their favorite books are, but be wary. Crowdsourcing is great for gathering information but it's dangerous for determining direction. It's best to use your network to collect information. Don't ask yes or no questions. Your friends will rarely tell you that you don't have a good idea. Also make sure your network is a valid source. Say you have a friend who loves hotels and he's always talking about hotels. But he has the worst taste in food ever. He is not a valid source on food.

▶ Voice is the number-one thing that excites me. When you meet someone who sounds different from other people—there is potential for greatness. The common denominator among Rocco, Jamie, Art Smith and Nigella? None of them sound like each other, and none of them sound like anyone else. And I don't just mean how they sound, literally. I mean how they view the world of cooking and food and how they express their knowledge and enthusiasm.

▶ My father's great lesson to me in business was that nobody buys a quarter-inch drill bit because they need a quarter-inch drill bit. They buy a quarter-inch drill bit because they need a quarter-inch *hole*. Solve a need. Ask yourself the hard question: Does this solve a need for anyone other than my need to write a book?

Once you have focused your direction and assembled your material, it is time to sit down and write your book proposal. A book proposal is more than an important selling tool, it spells out the true north of your book and will guide your writing each and every step of the way. Even if you already have a publisher interested, it's important to outline your book. Start a recipe list. Think about organization. Spend time figuring out your unique selling proposition. Have this at the ready for when the publisher comes calling.

Chapter 4

Proposals and Professionals Who Get Deals Done

❧❧

Nine times out of ten, selling a book to a publisher requires a proposal, or at the very least an outline. Even if you plan to self-publish, before you jump into writing your book, take the time to write a solid road map for your book. You should answer ALL of the important questions. What is your book about? Who is your book for? How do these consumers know about you? Why do they care? What is your unique culinary perspective? What is your unique voice? What will your book actually look like? How will your readers get their hands on the copies? A book proposal is usually more difficult to write than the actual book because it's where you have to do all of the hard work—unless you're very lucky and work with a publisher (like Page Street!) that prefers to work organically and develop a book and a target market at the same time. Even with a supportive and collaborative publisher, it's important to take stock of not just the tasks you love—developing recipes and telling stories—but also the tasks you might not love as much, like proving that you have something of value to share with the world. A good book proposal is proof of concept, and a smart author invests his or her energy in creating the best proposal he or she can. Because the better the proposal, the better the book, and the better the book deal.

A great proposal is grand on promise and specific in details. A great proposal paints the picture of the marketplace as well as your product. It illustrates how you are the perfect person to write this book and market it to the world. It showcases your best and brightest—only the rare books live up to the hype of the proposal. It is a selling tool and a wish list.

Andrew Friedman (www.toqueland.com), an author who has penned more than 40 cookbooks, explains the process this way:

◆ Unless you're somebody who is going to self-publish, you generally don't write your book until you've sold it. And to sell it, you need to do a few things. You need an agent to sell your book. If you're not somebody who is talented enough on the writing front or doesn't have the time to commit, you need a cowriter, or a collaborator or ghostwriter to get your voice on paper.

◆ Sometimes you can find an agent first, or a writer who you want to work with, and the two you of together find an agent.

◆ A proposal is a business plan in a lot of ways. A good proposal summarizes the viability of your concept, and in as much detail as possible, offers the Cliff's Notes version of the book, before it's written. It describes what the book will look like, sound like, and how it will be organized. After an agent or editor finishes the proposal, he or she should almost feel like he or she has read the book.

◆ Your proposal should include a Title Page and an Overview or Executive Summary, 8 to 20 pages that describe the pitch, in general terms. It states: this is who I am; this is my concept; why I am the right person to write it; and why you should buy it.

◆ You should also include an annotated table of contents, a list by chapter of the recipes that will be included, sample text and recipes including headnotes, little sidebars, and any supporting text.

◆ It's best to include tested recipes as well as at least one complete chapter introduction and supporting text.

◆ Traditionally proposals weren't art directed—just a word document—which was a lifeless way to sell something that would come to life with color photography. There's a bit of a shift happening, with more and more people submitting proposals that are art directed with a fully fleshed out art program to entice editors. These proposals make the book feel more immediate, and as it is much less expensive than it used to be to produce these, they are becoming standard.

List: Contents of a Great Proposal

1. Title page: includes title, subtitle, author's name, agent's name, date
2. Table of contents (of the proposal)
3. Overview/executive summary
4. About the author: your bio and photograph
5. Target market and how your book reaches them
6. Competitive analysis: A thorough look at competing titles and how your book is alike and different from them
7. Traditional publicity and marketing: what have you done and what are you going to do to market this book, including testimonials and sample media placements and a link to a reel of television appearances if your TV profile is your unique selling proposition.
8. Social media profile and platform (if substantial)
9. Design brief (if you're not handing in a designed proposal), including sample photographers and photos
10. Table of contents for the actual book
11. Complete list of recipes
12. Sample chapter, including sample tested recipes

Words of Wisdom

One of my favorite editors in the business, Justin Schwartz, who now is an executive editor at Houghton Mifflin Harcourt, gave me permission to include a hilariously brilliant, how-to post that he wrote on his personal blog, www.justcooknyc.com (he's worth a follow on Instagram too, especially if you're gluten-free):

1. This first entry is the inspiration for the post. **Don't send food in the mail** with your cookbook proposal unless you know the editor personally (or your agent does) and you're certain the recipient is at the office and will be receptive to it. If you *do* send food, make sure it's not highly perishable because it could be sitting in a mailroom for a while. Don't pack soft items in a padded envelope. And don't wrap the food in a mysterious tinfoil ball.

2. **Don't tell me about your grandmother's (mother's, aunt's, etc.) amazing recipes** and how you wrote the proposal because you want to preserve them for future generations. Everybody says this.

3. **Don't tell me you want to write a book because you have a lot of dinner parties and all your friends say how great your cooking is.** Everybody *else* says this.

4. **At the very least, don't send out a cookbook proposal** until you've read this post, *especially* if you're a blogger. I know authors who have already published books with major publishers who need to read that post.

5. **Don't send proposals with links to huge 50+ meg files** to download. And don't send eight attachments with one email. Send just one file, not too large, not packed with massive high-resolution photos on every page.

6. **Don't go the other direction** and send a one- or two-page cookbook proposal unless you're already a superstar (in which case you're probably not reading this post). A book title and list of chapters is not a proposal.

7. **Don't leave a photo of yourself out of the proposal**. I see a lot of bloggers who use logos or graphics for their avatar, but a publisher would be investing in you as a brand, and that's hard to do if you're hiding behind the scenes. Don't worry; you don't have to be a supermodel. Put your face out there.

8. Unless you take photos (like a professional) **don't fill your proposal with photography and insist on shooting the book yourself.** Shooting for print is much different from the web when everything is backlit on a computer screen, and sometimes mediocre photography can be the thing that costs you the deal, despite a great concept or wonderful recipes. On that subject, don't "design" the proposal unless you have real skills. Publishers will hire people to do that for you.

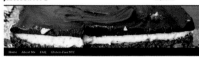

9. **Don't include photos of kids in your cookbook proposal**. Or to be more specific, don't Photoshop those kids into illustrated make-believe settings, dressed like characters from popular movies, cooking each other alive. It's incredibly creepy. Yes, this has really happened (more than once).

10. I don't care what those "get your book published" guidebooks say, **do not send your proposal to a publisher without a specific person's name on it**. Don't address it to the president or CEO of the company. And don't address it to "Mr. Harper Collins."

11. In fact, **don't try to navigate the world of publishing without an agent**. I'm pretty consistent about this advice. If you can't find an agent out of the hundreds of them to represent you, then you're going to have an impossible time finding a book publisher. A good agent knows all the editors and how to play by the rules. A good agent is your foot in the door and worth every penny.

12. **Don't tell me about your Twitter/Facebook/Pinterest/Instagram followers unless it's really worth mentioning**. If you have just 424 Twitter followers, you need to keep working on your social networking strategy before trying to sell a book (or doing any kind of business, quite frankly) because your community is probably still just your personal network of friends. Have you seen the funny SNL video "You Can Do Anything"? If you haven't, google it. This is what I think of when someone sends me a proposal with a link to their Facebook fan page with almost no following.

13. On that subject, **don't tell me about your website that you haven't launched yet** or have links on your blog to sister sites or social networking platforms that are not up and running. Sure, you came up with a great idea and bought a URL for it, but that's not enough to attract a publisher. We want to see traffic, steady growth, followers and lots of comments. We want to see the community you've built over time.

14. **Don't write a post about bacon on your blog the same week you send out a vegetarian cookbook proposal** to every editor in the business. On that subject, seriously, don't try to sell a proposal that has nothing to do with your platform or reputation. I'm a big believer in specialization. If your website about gluten-free food gets 100,000 views a month, that's much better than a general-interest food blog which gets 200,000 views a month. I could write a long post about this subject to explain it better, but just trust me for now. Also on this subject, if you claim to be an active blogger, you'd better be posting more often than twice a month.

15. **Don't specialize too much.** Gluten-free, vegetarian, low-fat and pressure cooking are great categories, but not all in one book. And I may have broken this rule myself before, but just because there is nothing published on a given subject (*The Best Carrot Recipes Ever!*), it **doesn't mean there is a void in the cookbook category that needs to be filled**. If you think there is a void, at the least you should try blogging about the subject first to test out your logic.

16. Just because you write about Italian food, **don't compare yourself in the proposal to Giada**. Or just because you're crafty or love entertaining, don't claim to be the new Martha unless you have a huge following of some kind. I know this is tough advice, but *everybody* says these kinds of things in *every* proposal I see. Focus on being yourself.

17. Speaking of TV stars, **don't promise you're starring in your own TV series** until it's a done deal. I can't count how many people, including many of my current authors, have been approached by TV producers, shot pilots (or even a few episodes), and waited months or years, without luck, for those shows to be sold to a network. In fact, any publisher would rather wait for the show to start airing and pay you a lot more money to write a book if the show is a hit. You'll also likely have agents begging to represent you if the TV deal goes through.

18. **Don't assume your ninth-place finish on Season 7 of that cable TV show means anything to a publisher.** I guess it's better than nothing, but *everybody* who appears on those shows is trying to write a cookbook. If you're lucky enough to be on a show like that, you'd better at least make sure you were really memorable, preferably not for being a jerk or drama queen.

19. This is a long one—**don't be inconsiderate**. You know the old joke about meeting a doctor at a cocktail party and asking him to look at that weird mole, or meeting a lawyer and asking her for some impromptu legal advice. It's a little annoying for them. Cookbook editors (or agents) at writer/blogger conferences are fair game—of course you should try to meet them. Find a comfortable way to introduce yourself or be introduced, hand them a card (you have business cards, right?), make your elevator pitch if you can, and then read the signals. If the editor asks questions in response, then great. If they politely offer to check out your site and then excuse themselves from the conversation, respect that. If it's a social event where you're meeting, try to be a little more understanding. They might be there to have fun. Don't keep pulling them away from their friends, interrupting conversations and going on and on about your passion for food and your whole life story unless you want to risk burning bridges. See if the editor is doing a "meet the pros" session and sign up for that, or if the editor is speaking on a panel about publishing, try to introduce yourself after it's over. Believe it or not, I speak on those kinds of panels because I want people to pitch me book ideas. But at a random weekend meet-up among local bloggers, I might just be out to have a good time.

20. This is a weird one, but if you do meet or get to know an editor, **don't ask them to take an early look at your proposal unless you're offering them exclusivity**. I imagine some agents won't agree with me about this, but when I see a not-quite-finished proposal, if I like it, I might give the writer some advice. If you take that advice and then try selling the improved proposal to another editor, well, it's really not cool.

21. If you have great recipes but your writing isn't very strong, **don't try to do it yourself**. Even the pros use cowriters. A proposal full of typographical errors is going to get rejected, no matter how great the recipes might be. By the way, a good agent won't let you make these kinds of mistakes.

22. That being said, **don't send your proposal to an editor until it's the best it can be**. You might not get another shot at this. Take the extra time to build your platform, hone your craft, and make the proposal something you're proud of. I'm sure there is some applicable cliché about how "winners are doers" and that kind of thing, but I like another cliché—"patience is a virtue." Just because your best friends keep telling you how great you are on Twitter, it doesn't mean you're ready for the big leagues. Take the time to get it right. Seek feedback beyond your personal network. Push your boundaries. Attend a conference or two. Work with a mentor. Keep writing that blog (or for bigger websites or print publications) and building your platform. Take a writing class or a photography class. Embrace social networking. Invest in yourself before you take the next big step.

Your Cookbook Team

Hillary Clinton tells us that to succeed in life it takes a village. Writing a cookbook can take a village, too. Publishers don't expect bloggers or chefs or especially celebrities to be experts at all the skills needed to write a great cookbook. Most authors assemble a team of people to help them produce their book, in addition to the team that their publisher provides. At the proposal stage, you will want to consider adding a writer and recipe tester to your team. If you are doing the writing yourself, it is worth investing in a copy editor to review your work. If you want to submit a designed proposal, then you need to hire a designer. DIY does not always win the day. Your agent will have a list of people he or she likes to work with and will make recommendations based on your budget and compatibility. I can't stress enough that the proposal is the first major investment in your future.

How do I find a literary agent?

At least once a week someone asks me to recommend a literary agent. A good literary agent is an expert in the marketplace and will guide your publishing career with each individual book and your trajectory as a whole. They know every publisher, big and small, what the going rate for a similar title is, who will be most likely to buy your copy, they host auctions, collect and distribute your money and are worth every penny of the 15 percent they charge. They take new clients on faith and invest their energy and relationships into helping you build your literary brand. Next to being a publicist, it's the hardest job in publishing. Unlike editors, literary agents receive unsolicited proposals all of the time—but that's probably the hardest way to find an agent.

My agent is David Black, founder of the David Black Agency, and I consider myself one of the luckiest girls in the game. Part shrink, part psychic, part Warren Buffett (did I mention he's also Warren Buffett's agent?) and sprinkled with just enough Ari Gold, David will read your material and within five minutes tell you if he can sell it or not. But more importantly, he will then tell you how to refine your proposal to make it more marketable. And David Black, like most agents of his caliber, is very picky about his clients. He doesn't get paid unless he makes a sale, so for him choosing wisely is the key to his future success.

If your proposal gets picked up by an agent—you've made it past the first hurdle in the traditional publishing process. (Of course it's important to mention that there are also untraditional publishing routes. You can get lucky and publish without an agent at all, and Chapter Ten explains the pros and cons of self-publishing—right now, though, we're old school.) Write a proposal, find an agent, sell a book to a publisher, publish a book. I imagine a time in the not-too-distant future where it will look more like: post a photo on Instagram, reply to the comment, get a book deal. In 2015, that is the exception to the rule—but the game is changing fast. The smart money hedges its bets, and does both—works on a traditional proposal, while tweeting and Instagramming and engaging with a large following of people.

My favorite advice on finding an agent comes from Ann Bramson, publisher of Artisan Books. She recommends going to the bookstore and pulling together a pile of cookbooks that you love or believe to be similar to yours. Scour the acknowledgements for the agent's name. Send them a note with your proposal asking for representation. It's much easier now than ever, though, to find someone you know to make an introduction. Use LinkedIn or Facebook to find mutual friends and then ask for a favor of introduction. Check out www.writersdigest.com, a site that offers a listing of agents and their specialties.

Words of Wisdom:
Pam Krauss

Pam Krauss has been in the cookbook publishing business for close to 30 years as one of its most successful editors and publishers. She's published hundreds of bestselling cookbook authors, including the biggest names today such as Rachael Ray, Ina Garten, Giada DeLaurentiis, Mario Batali, Mark Bittman, Alicia Silverstone, Alice Waters, Bobby Flay, Martha Stewart and Tricia Yearwood, to name a few. She can make great cookbooks from as little as a great title or as much as 1,000 recipes that she has to wade and weed through to get down to a manageable size. She's ridden the rise of Food Network stars, Internet stars and every dietary trend or celebrity idea out there, not by depending on the name recognition alone but by creating quality books with recipes that work and pictures that delight. She's never been one to mince words, and when asked for some words of wisdom on proposals, she delivered on her reputation.

- Every once in a great while I get wowed by a proposal, a piece of work that really showcases an idea and truly understands what else is out there in the marketplace. I hate it when people say there is no other book out there, when there clearly is, and we've actually published it 18 months ago!

- Authors need to understand who their audience is. Everybody means nobody. We look for very specific and targeted demographics. Give examples of where these people look for recipes and can't find enough or want more variety. And then demonstrate the demand for your recipes and brand.

- I ask three very basic questions: Why me? Why this? Why now?

- Cookbooks should have an easy-to-understand premise. I am forever chiding my team that if we have to tell too much of a story with our jacket design or our titles then people probably won't want the book.

- The art of writing a great recipe is not lost. If you open up a proposal and see 80 recipes that you really want to publish—you buy that book.

- If you have a strong presence on Pinterest that could be a way in and will catch our attention. If you ask a 23-year-old what their favorite cooking site is, they will answer Pinterest.

The Money

The only information people want more than agent names are going rates. What do cookbooks sell for these days? The answer, of course, is obvious. It widely varies from very little, i.e., less than $8,000, to much more than could ever be earned back. Think of an advance like a gamble for the publisher. They are betting you are going to make them money. The bigger bet they place, the more faith (and proof) they need to have that you will earn the advance they have paid you. Typically, smaller publishers will offer $4,000 to $6,000. The upside of this is that smaller publishers are willing to place small bets on untested talent. Bigger publishers (with bigger advances) can't afford to be wrong, so they therefore set the acquisition bar much higher and place strong demands on the authors. When evaluating a proposal, a publisher will do a profit-and-loss statement for the book. They put in all of the fixed costs, from cost of acquisition and actual printing, to design, photography and marketing, and then run the numbers to see how many copies they will need to sell to earn back the advance on the book. Traditional publishing runs on essentially a consignment model. The publisher advances you an amount of money to write the book, and then you earn it back at publication. Once the advance is earned back (one reason that small advances aren't so horrible—and have the potential for a big upside even when you sell fewer copies), you start earning a royalty percentage for each copy sold. The more copies sold, the more money you make. Let's do the math. Your publisher advances you $10,000 for your first cookbook. It's a paperback original and they set the price at $22.00 and a royalty of 10 percent of the retail price. For each book sold, you get a $2.20 credit toward your $10,000 debt. To earn out, you need to sell 4,546 books. At the 4,547th book, you start earning a $2.20 credit into your account. Twice a year, your publisher reconciles your account and cuts you a check. If you sell 10,000 books in the first year, then you earn $11,998.80 (less your agent's percentage, if you have one) in royalties.

It's the rare cookbook that will make you a millionaire. Most authors have "day jobs" to supplement the book income. So please don't go quitting your day job until you have started selling books. It's also important to mention that the business of writing a cookbook is an expensive one. You have to purchase all of the food to actually test each recipe multiple times to guarantee a good result. You might also have to hire some help on both the writing and testing and might even have to pay for the photographer out of your advance. Again, each publisher has a different formula. Some publishers offer an art budget (to cover photography and food costs) and some publishers hire the team directly and cover all of the costs. Before you embark on the process, you should do a profit-and-loss statement for yourself to figure out how much the book will cost you to write and how many copies you need to sell to make it a worthwhile investment of time.

Of course, keep in mind that with no risk there is no reward, so let's move on to creating this masterpiece. It's time to setup the computer in the kitchen and get to work.

PART TWO

Creating

Chapter 5

Write, Test, Repeat

Now that it's time to get to work, you really need to grasp the importance of the actual recipes you will be creating. Recipes should never be throwaway components of your cookbook—some dishes that can be whipped up quickly and soon forgotten. They are the way to showcase your voice and let the reader see what sets your ideas apart from everybody else's. As cookbook veteran Christopher Styler explains, what makes a recipe original is that it's "an unusual combination of flavor, techniques and ingredients." And getting them 100 percent accurate and easy-to-follow is your number-one responsibility to readers.

Sure, many chefs become famous by demonstrating how to grill the perfect burger on late-night TV, but if you disappoint your readers when they're trying out one of your recipes at home, you're probably not going to get another shot at their attention—or their wallet. Remember, home cooks are relying on you to show them how to make a meal that's important to them—be it a first date, a healthy dinner for four on the fly after a hectic day at the office or an elaborate holiday meal for the entire extended family (especially that oh-so-hard-to-please mother-in-law or food blogging, Instagramming cousin). These readers don't need to see you show off *your* chops in the kitchen as much as they need you to teach them how to make a meal special, delicious and foolproof so that they can impress the people in their life.

So, where to begin?

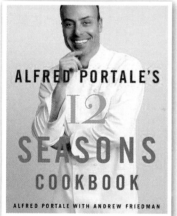

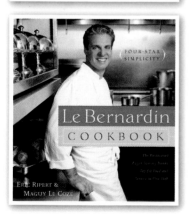

First, look for some inspiration. A good place to start is the cookbook section of your favorite bookstore. Peruse the shelves to find what style makes you feel most excited to step into the kitchen.

Andrew Friedman recalls finding inspiration from renowned San Francisco chef Paul Bertolli when he worked with Alfred Portale of Gotham Bar & Grill on his first book. "I asked [Alfred] to give me a book he really respected. He had me google *Chez Panisse Cooking* that Paul Bertolli cowrote. The headnotes were amazing. They weren't what I thought of as a cookbook. They were essays on ingredients." Friedman and Portale used that book as their muse when cowriting their second book, Alfred Portale's *12 Seasons Cookbook*, which they organized month-by-month, sharing seasonal recipes that *Publishers Weekly* raved brought "together bold flavors in unexpected ways, as in 'Seared Foie Gras with Poached Quince, Tangerine and Pomegranate Juice.' ... and though many recipes require multiple building blocks, it is not beyond the reach of enthusiastic cooks. The directions are clearly presented, even for such challenging fare as 'Soupe de Poisson and Trout Wrapped in Bacon with Braised Escarole, Green Lentils, Sage and Sherry Vinaigrette.'"

That review tells you Portale and Friedman successfully pulled off a serious cookbook, translating the mechanics of a 4-star professional kitchen for the layperson. But you'll notice that's definitely not the only type of cookbook available today. And now would be a very good time to figure out which one you're most suited to write. Below are three wildly different recipe styles.

1. The Professional: These recipes are the fanciest of the crop. They typically use a lot of French terms, classic techniques performed in the best professional kitchens and a lot of precise steps. Someone who follows one of these recipes will feel like they've spent a day attending classes at the Culinary Institute of America. In this sample recipe from 4-star chef Eric Ripert of Le Bernardin you will notice technique, technique, technique (even in the headnote). That's what separates the pros from the home cooks, as well as the language that professional cooks use (julienne for slice thinly, dice for chop, etc.), the equipment that only professional cooks would use (circle cutters, sizzle pans and chinois, to name a few) and hard-to-find ingredients that usually require mail order. And each recipe usually contains at least distinct component recipes needed to create the dish. Most of these chef books are destined to become "coffee-table" books—big, beautiful tomes that we love to keep out to impress our friends and show our foodie cred ("I picked that up when I ate at The French Laundry, Thomas Keller signed it for us at the table"), but are rarely found in the kitchen.

Spotlight:

Eric Ripert's Poached Halibut, Sweet-and-Sour Golden and Red Beets and Citrus-Coriander Oil Emulsion

I picked up this poaching technique from my friend Laurent Gras, who learned it from a Chinese chef. Cooking a delicate fish like halibut in a thick veloute lets the fish retain its moistness and gives it a wonderful glossiness.

Tip: Start citrus-coriander oil one day in advance

Serves 4

SWEET-AND-SOUR BEETS
2 cups red wine vinegar
1 cup sherry vinegar
4 cups water
½ cup kosher salt
2 medium golden beets
2 medium red beets
Fine sea salt and freshly ground white pepper
2 tbsp infused citrus-coriander oil (recipe follows)

CITRUS-CORIANDER OIL EMULSION
¼ cup fresh orange juice
2 tbsp fresh lemon juice
2 tbsp ponzu (see below)
2 tsp minced shallot
½ cup infused citrus-coriander oil (recipe follows)
Fine sea salt and freshly ground white pepper
Espelette pepper powder

THE POACHING LIQUID
4 tbsp unsalted butter
¼ cup all-purpose flour
7 cups water
½ cup fresh orange juice
½ cup fresh lemon juice
1 tbsp vermouth
Fine sea salt

THE HALIBUT
4 6-oz halibut fillets
Fine sea salt and freshly ground white pepper

GARNISH
1 tbsp basil julienne
1 tbsp opal basil julienne

For the beets, divide the vinegars, water and kosher salt between two medium saucepans. Add the golden beets to one pan and the red beets to the other. Bring to a boil, then reduce the heat slightly and cook the beets until tender, 45 to 60 minutes. Drain the beets and let cool.

Peel the beets and cut them into ¼-inch-thick slices. You need 16 yellow beet slices and 12 red beet slices. Using a 1½-inch round cutter, trim each slice into a neat circle. Lay the beet circles on a parchment-lined baking sheet. (The beets can be cooked and sliced ahead of time and kept refrigerated until ready to use.)

For the citrus-coriander oil emulsion, combine the orange juice, lemon juice, ponzu and shallot in a small stainless steel saucepan and bring to a simmer. Whisking constantly, drizzle in the oil in a steady stream. Season to taste with salt, white pepper and Espelette pepper. Keep warm.

For the poaching liquid, melt the butter in a small pot over medium heat. Add the flour and stir with a wooden spoon until the mixture is smooth. Cook the roux, stirring constantly, until it is a golden straw color and has a slightly nutty aroma, about 5 minutes. Remove from the heat and let cool to prevent lumps when you add the roux to the hot liquid.

Bring the water to a boil in a medium pot. Add the orange juice, lemon juice, and vermouth and bring back to a boil. Whisking constantly, add half of the roux. Add the rest of the roux and bring to a boil (the mixture will look like a thick soup). Season with salt and simmer until all the raw flour taste has cooked out, about 15 minutes.

Reduce the heat and let the poaching liquid cool to 180°F, just under a simmer. Simmer for a few more minutes to cook the acidity out, whisking the liquid occasionally to prevent a skin from forming.

Preheat the oven to 350°F.

For the halibut, transfer the liquid to a shallow pan. Season the fillets on both sides with salt and pepper. Place them in the poaching liquid and poach for 5 to 6 minutes, turning once, until a metal skewer can be easily inserted into the fish and, if left in for 5 seconds, feels just warm when touched to your lip.

While the fish is poaching, season the beets with salt and white pepper and drizzle the citrus-coriander oil over them. Heat the beets in the oven until they are warm, about 2 minutes.

To serve, remove the halibut from the poaching liquid and drain on a towel. Arrange four golden beet slices and three red beet slices in a circle in the center of each plate, alternating red and yellow slices. Place the halibut on top of the beets and garnish with the basil julienne. Spoon the citrus emulsion over and around the halibut, and serve immediately.

(continued)

INFUSED CITRUS-CORIANDER OIL
Grated zest of 1 orange
Grated zest of 1 lemon
2 tbsp fennel seeds
2 tbsp coriander seeds
½ star anise
3 basil sprigs
2 cilantro sprigs
1 tomato, cored and chopped
1 cup olive oil
½ cup extra virgin olive oil
¼ cup lemon oil
Fine sea salt

Crush the orange zest, lemon zest, fennel seeds, coriander seeds, star anise, basil, cilantro, and tomato together in a bowl. Add the three oils and season well with salt. Cover with plastic wrap and refrigerate for 24 hours or up to 10 days.

To use, gently warm the oil and strain it through a fine-mesh sieve; discard the aromatics.

Ponzu

Makes about 3 ½ cups

1 cup soy sauce
Minced zest and juice of ½ orange
Minced zest and juice of ½ lemon
Minced zest and juice of ¼ lime
⅓ cup yuzu juice
1 teaspoon sugar
2 cups water

Mix all of the ingredients together in a bowl. Transfer to a jar or bottle, seal tightly, and refrigerate for at least 24 hours before using.

2. The Molecular Gastronomist: This is a book written by chefs who love to geek out over the science behind cooking. It's heavy on step-by-step photos and instructions on how to use the latest kitchen gadgets (think smoking guns, homogenizers, thermal immersion blenders, sous vide machines and even a centrifuge!). The reader will feel like the smartest kid in the kitchen after successfully mastering one of these recipes.

Most famously, Nathan Myhrvold won a James Beard cookbook award in 2012 for his six-volume tome, *Modernist Cuisine: The Art and Science of Cooking*. The work, inspired by Myhrvold's desire to understand the technique of sous vide cooking, breaks down the process of cooking right down to exactly what heat does to food. As Myhrvold told NOVA in 2011, "We aren't just trying to do our grandma's recipes. We're trying to focus on understanding the scientific basis for what is this thing we call cooking."

Myhrvold is exploring what most of us call molecular gastronomy, practiced first and perhaps most famously by superstar Spanish chef Ferran Adrià. This is most likely not the kind of book you will be writing, unless you've spent the last 15 years in the kitchens of Adrià or Dane Rene Redzepi or American Grant Achatz. Or you're a retired Microsoft millionaire who is looking for a new hobby.

3. The Novelist: Think heaps of personality and memorable prose. The chef leisurely walks you through his or her thought process as well as past experiences at the stove. By the end, the reader practically feels like they're taking direction from a close friend or family member.

Bee Wilson, the author of *Consider the Fork*, best describes this type of recipe in her 2013 *New Yorker* article titled, "The Pleasure of Reading Recipes."

> "Recipe readers are always talking about how cookbooks are like novels, and there's a clue here to how we actually read them. Like a short story, a good recipe can put us in a delightful trance. The *Oxford English Dictionary* defines fiction as literature 'concerned with the narration of imaginary events.' This is what recipes are: stories of pretend meals. Don't be fooled by the fact that they are written in the imperative tense (pick the basil leaves, peel the onion). Yes, you might do that tomorrow, but right now, you are doing something else. As you read, your head drowsily on the pillow, there is no onion but you watch yourself peel it in your mind's eye, tugging off the papery skin and noting with satisfaction that you have not damaged the layers underneath."

Wilson adds, "Recipes have a story arc. You need to get through the tricky early prepping stages via the complications of heat and measuring before you arrive at the point of happy closure where the dish goes in the oven or is sliced or served. When a recipe has many ingredients and stages and finicky instructions, it can be hard to concentrate, like reading a Victorian novel with so many characters that you need a *dramatis personae* to keep things straight."

British chef Nigella Lawson is one of my absolute favorites in this category. Her seductive personality pours onto the page with every direction and tip. She "tumbles in olives" instead of just throwing them into a pot and "gives sauce a swirl" instead of merely mixing in a pan. You practically feel like you're dancing in the kitchen with her guidance. Check out her recipe for Crème Brûleé.

Spotlight:
Nigella Lawson's Crème Brûlée

The first thing you should know about Crème Brûlée is that it's not hard to make. And few puddings are as voluptuously, seductively easy to eat. I never make mine in little individual ramekins (though there's nothing to stop you if that's what you prefer) but in one large dish—there is something so welcoming about a big bowlful, the rich, smooth, eggy cream waiting to ooze out on the spoon that breaks through the tortoiseshell disc on top.

600 mL double cream
1 vanilla pod
8 large egg yolks
3 tablespoons caster sugar
Approximately 6 tbsp Demerara sugar

Put a pie dish of about 8 inches/20 centimeters diameter in the freezer for at least 20 minutes. Half-fill the sink with cold water. This is just a precaution in case the custard looks as if it's about to split, in which case you should plunge the pan into the water and whisk the custard. I'm not saying it will—with so many egg yolks in the rich cream, it thickens quickly and easily enough—but I always feel better if I've done this.

Put the cream and vanilla pod into a saucepan and bring to the boiling point, but do not let boil. Beat the eggs and caster sugar together in a bowl and, still beating, pour the flavored cream over it, pod and all. Rinse and dry the pan and pour the custard mix back in. Cook over medium heat (or low, if you're scared) until the custard thickens—about 10 minutes should do it. You do want this to be a good, voluptuous creme, so don't err on the side of runny caution. Remember, you've got your sink full of cold water to plunge the pan into should it really look as if it's about to split.

When the cream's thick enough, take out the vanilla pod, retrieve the pie dish and pour this creme into the severely chilled container. Leave to cool, then put in the fridge till truly cold. Sprinkle with Demerara sugar, spoonful by spoonful, and burn with a blowtorch till you have a blistered tortoiseshell covering on top.

Put back in the fridge if you want, but remember to take it out a good 20 minutes before serving. At which stage, put the bowl on the table and, with a large spoon and unchecked greed, crack through the sugary carapace and delve into the satin-velvet, vanilla-speckled cream beneath. No more talking; just eat.

Copyright 2002. Reprinted with permission Hachette books.

Very few people can write like Nigella. None in fact, so I don't recommend you try. What I do recommend is that you find a style that works for you. Jamie Oliver has perfected the casual recipe writing style—he measures in glugs and drops and pinches and teacupfuls. He's trying to build confidence in the kitchen by taking all of the scary stuff out. Most cookbook writers go for the straightforward approach when writing recipes—add water and stir. In fact, it's probably best to start with the simplest instructions possible on paper and then go into the kitchen and build on what you've written. Details and descriptions are your friends. When in doubt, err on the side of precision.

Regardless of which style you choose to write, all recipes should meet certain expectations and be usable by ANY level home chef. They should be unique, easy to follow and worth repeating time and again. They should also include three key components in their structure. 1) A headnote—that brief blurb at the top of the page that describes what people can expect from the recipe. 2) A list of every ingredient needed for the dish. 3) Concise directions on your methodology of preparing and cooking.

While some media outlets debate the necessity of headnotes, I believe it's really the way to share your distinctive voice with the reader. This is where you will entice them by telling them how the dish will taste, look and smell. It can also include a personal anecdote about what the dish means to you, advice on when to serve and how to apply what they'll learn in this recipe to other dishes.

Below are some of my favorite writers of headnotes.

Award-winning cookbook author Mollie Katzen (originally known for the legendary Moosewood Restaurant) writes headnotes that are simple but sublime and informative. In the headnote for her "Arizona Pumpkin Soup" in *The New Enchanted Broccoli Forest* cookbook, she writes: "Tart and tangy, this easy pumpkin soup goes beautifully with fresh, warm tortillas and a spinach salad for a quick and cozy autumn dinner. You can bake a pumpkin, but canned works just as well. (Try canned organic pumpkin! It's worth looking for.) Canned pumpkin will enable you to enjoy a steaming bowlful of soup just 30 minutes after you begin to cook. **NOTE:** You can substitute baked winter squash or sweet potatoes for the pumpkin."

So does Barbara Kafka, the renowned food writer and most recently author of *The Intolerant Gourmet*. In her recipe for "Spiffy French Country Paté" she writes:

> "This is a quick and fairly easy pâté that needs to be made ahead but then keeps in the refrigerator—well wrapped—for almost a week. It actually improves in flavor with time. It is a godsend for dinner parties and cocktail parties as it can be made ahead and served with mustard and cornichons (tiny pickles) and either crackers and bread or on salad leaves—watercress and/or spinach do particularly well. This is one of the first recipes I have tested in a 1,200-watt oven."

I also love when chefs feel free to indulge in a longer story like Food Network star Alex Guarnaschelli does when introducing her recipe for her mom's meat loaf in her 2013 book, *Old-School Comfort Food*.

> "On the corner of my block was this old Irish bar, Mulligan's. Sometimes I would see the cooks there slicing big thick wedges of meat loaf and it made me want to grab two oversize slices of crusty bread and make a sandwich. My mother's tiny meat loaf paled in comparison the first time I saw her pull it from the oven. It didn't have that oversize look but I smiled politely as she cut me a small piece. Then I took a bite. Ketchup? Yes. Tarragon and sour cream? Stokes of genius. My meat loaf allegiance was forever changed. If you have time, grind your own beef, using brisket and chuck, and your own pork, using a shoulder cut. I will admit that I get a meat loaf that is slightly lighter and the meat is easier to work with."

Words of Wisdom:
The Art of the Headnote

Prolific cookbook collaborator Andrew Friedman's philosophy on headnotes stems from his first cowriting experience with Alfred Portale of the Gotham Bar & Grill. "He really wanted long headnotes," recalls Friedman. "There was a symbiotic relationship between the headnote and the recipe. He didn't just introduce and go home. He made you want to look back." He offers us his words of wisdom on the art of the headnote.

▷ **Make it literary.** "I am still shocked at the number of people who sit in bed and read headnotes like novels," he says. "To me, a really good headnote tells you everything worth knowing about technique, ingredients and your personal story."

➡ **Keep it short.** "Very short declarative sentences are much better than long, flowing sentences to get your point across," he says. Think of your headnote like a brief toast. "Good speech writing is very short, simple sentences strung together."

➡ **But go big**. "When you put your thoughts on paper, your speech inflection, tone of voice and gestures don't make it onto the page. To get your personality across, you need to compensate with words."

➡ **Ask for help**. Can't perfect your voice? Get a collaborator to help you bring it out. Just don't think that's taking the easy way out. "You still have to put in the time," reminds Friedman. "You can't just point and shoot. You need to say I wouldn't use this word, or I would build out that point more."

Next up is creating a list of ingredients. This step may seem much easier than it actually is. Many home chefs can stumble if the list isn't perfect. Be sure to include every ingredient the recipe calls for—even if you think it's a household staple everyone already has in the pantry. There is nothing more frustrating to a home cook than discovering they don't have enough garlic powder required for the dish when they get to step 4 because garlic powder wasn't on the original ingredient list.

Be sure to list the ingredients in order of use so that a home cook can perfect the art of mise en place. This practice has been used for years in professional kitchens but it's just as effective in the home kitchen. And don't forget to add the correct number of servings at the top of your directions!

Of course, all this may seem fundamental to someone who works in the kitchen, but being a good cook is one thing; teaching others how to be a good cook is an entirely different skill set.

BBC's Good Food website offers a few more nuggets of advice to help you compile a great recipe:

➡ Seasonality is the key for achieving the most flavorsome results, says assistant editor Cassie Best. "When thinking of recipe ideas I tend to start with what's in season, then from this I'll think of what flavors lend themselves well to these foods."

➡ Balance of ingredients is also important. Former BBC Good Food cookery assistant Adam Russell recommends building a recipe from a base to get the right balance of flavors. "First look at the flavors that work well together as a foundation," he says. "Then experiment with their quantities to get the right balance, so that they complement instead of overpower each other."

FOOD52

Spotlight: *Amanda Hesser*

Of course, nowadays a cookbook writer who can adapt to the changing times can go very far. Amanda Hesser—and her evolution in the culinary world—is a great example of that. In the early 1990s she lived in Europe and thought about becoming a bread baker until, in her words, she "fell into writing." During her 11 years at *The New York Times*, she reported on the food industry, had recipe columns and cowrote *The Essential New York Times Cookbook*. Her recipes were perfect specimens of precision and detail. She also never became complacent about her job skills. "I tried to do as many different creative and entrepreneurial things as I could and not be so entrenched in reporting and writing," she told me.

In 2007, that involved perfecting her delicious narrative style of food writing with her bestselling book *Cooking for Mr. Latte*, which interspersed recipes with delightful first-person prose about dating—and cooking for—her future husband. Next up? The forefront of the digital revolution. In 2008, she began developing Food52, an award-winning website where home cooks can share their best recipes, with Merrill Stubbs. So now she helps other people hone their specific recipe styles.

"We want all of the recipes to have great personal character," Hesser explains. "I personally like authors who are very good reads and not just offering sterile instruction. They have your back and get you excited about cooking for pleasure."

Below are some of her favorite cookbook writers:

 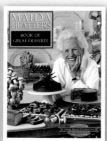

➡ Carol Field, author of the award-winning *The Italian Baker*: She wrote about history and craftsmanship.

➡ Maida Heatter, author of *Maida Heatter's Book of Great Desserts*: She was straight up. You always feel like she's looking over your shoulder and worrying about what you're worrying about

➡ Nigella Lawson and Fergus Henderson: They infuse their recipes with personality, energy and wit. I learned from them that you can describe something thoroughly without it being dry.

Words of Wisdom:
Recipe Writing Tips From Christopher Styler

For more than 20 years, chef and cookbook writer Christopher Styler (www.chrisstyler.com) has been my go-to guy in the kitchen. He has a calm presence in even the most chaotic situations. He has developed and tested at least 4,500 recipes for books, magazines and corporations over the years and has learned a thing or two about how to get a good one down on the page. Here are some of his best tips:

▷ It's good to have an idea of why you go into the kitchen and what you plan to come out with but try very hard not have any preconceived ideas—for example, I was recently developing recipes for a piece of equipment that I had never used before. I assumed that the heating element on the machine would work the same way a pot on a stove would. Boy, was I bummed when I realized that none of the timings I had mapped out were right and literally had to test each recipe six times before I got close to a repeatable result.

▷ Write in English, not in recipe-ese. As much information as possible should be in really easy language. You should be very clear about how to treat, clean, prepare and cook every ingredient. The reader reviews I'm proudest of always say "the directions are incredibly clear and very helpful."

▷ Assume nothing except that the people you are writing for need some kind of guidance. I don't mean that in an insulting way but in a way that assumes they are not professional chefs. Any little tidbit you can give them is really helpful. Tell them how the fish cooking should look, feel and smell. Is the skin supposed to be brown and crispy? Then tell them. Is the fish supposed to be opaque and spring back to the touch? Tell them. If the liquid in the pan could evaporate before the fish finishes cooking, causing it to burn, make sure you tell them to keep an eye on the pan and add water as necessary. Remember all pans and stoves are different. You have to warn for potential pitfalls otherwise your poor readers are going to fall right into them.

▷ Know your audience. "How much money do they want to spend, how much time do they want to cook?" The answers to these questions will totally inform what kind of recipes you write. If you are writing for busy moms, and your recipe calls for exotic ingredients and multiple preparations and lots of different equipment (that will require lots of washing after dinner!), then you're most likely to have a very unhappy customer.

Keep your knives sharp.... Above all, have a good time. While you're in the kitchen developing recipes, it's critical to be as observant as possible in order to avoid problems down the road. Time every single step. Jot down what things feel and smell like along the way. We've already established that you will need to give readers as many helpful visual and sensory clues as possible.

But even that is not enough. Making sure your recipes have been tested over and over again is essential to writing a solid cookbook. Christopher Kimball, the founder of *Cook's Illustrated*, proudly touts on their website that they typically use 50 cooks and test a recipe 50 to 100 times. "We make the mistakes so you don't have to," he says. That should be your motto, too.

Of course, you should have a professional tester on your team, but crowdsourcing is another good way to gage the reliability of one of your recipes. Ask six friends to try out your recipes. Make sure they are all at different levels—two excellent chefs, two average ones and two complete novices who get flustered by making toast. And ask them to carefully record their results. Where were they nervous in the process? What did the finished dish look like? How did it taste? Did the recipe deliver on the promise in the headnote? Did they enjoy cooking the recipe? Would they want to make it again?

A Quick History Lesson
Julia Child: Mastering the Art of Writing a Cookbook

Of course, no guide to writing a cookbook would be worth its weight in salt without mentioning Julia Child, the consummate queen of cooking. She starred in award-winning TV shows, wrote bestselling cookbooks (plus one beloved memoir) and became the first female to be inducted into the Culinary Institute Hall of Fame.

Her initial claim to fame though was demystifying the techniques behind complex French dishes for regular Americans in a groundbreaking cookbook. *Mastering the Art of French Cooking*; published in 1961, it inspired novice chefs across the country at a time when most people found making an omelet daunting. The book's success is all the more impressive considering Child confessed to having "zero interest in the stove" as a child and didn't get serious about cooking until the age of 37.

By now, her story is well-known. After a privileged childhood in Pasadena, California, and a successful career as a research assistant for the government intelligence agency OSS, she moved to France with her beloved husband Paul in 1948. The following year, she began attending a yearlong course at Le Cordon Bleu and ultimately collaborated with Simone Beck and Louisette Bertholle on a two-volume cookbook that taught the essential techniques of French cooking—and translated them for the home cook in America. It took the trio a decade to finish the book. The women were paid an advance of $750 for the book but the initial publisher rejected the manuscript because of its length (over 600 pages).

Instead, Judith Jones, an editor for Knopf, who had pushed for publication of Anne Frank's diary, discovered the manuscript and predicted it would become a classic.

Jones's notes about the manuscript, available on RandomHouse.com, reveal the secret to the book's success.

> "I've had this French cookbook for Americans for almost two months now, have read it through, tried innumerable recipes, some simple and some challenging, and I think it's not only first-rate but unique. I don't know of another book that succeeds so well in defining and translating for Americans the secrets of French cuisine. The reason? Because the authors emphasize technique—not the number of recipes they can cram into a volume, nor the exotic nature of the dishes. Reading and studying this book seems to me as good as taking a basic course at the Cordon Bleu. Actually it's better than that because the authors' whole focus is on how to translate the tricks learned to the problems that confront you at home (i.e., the differences in meat cuts, utensils, materials). It is not a book for the lazy but for the cook who wants to improve, to take that giant step from fair-to-good accomplishment to that subtle perfection that makes French cooking an art. I swear that I learned something from this manuscript every few pages.

(continued)

As to recipes, they have very intelligently selected the dishes that are really the backbone of the classic cuisine. The approach is to introduce the general subject first: what to look for in buying, best utensil to use, timing, testing for doneness, tricks to improve. Then there is usually a master recipe, presented in painstaking detail, followed by variations, different choices of sauces for embellishing the same dish. There is a good deal of text devoted not to cuisine lore but to practical detail; you are seldom directed to do something without being told why. The authors are perfectionists, opinionated, and culinary snobs in the best sense—that is, they will approve of a frozen short cut, when time demands it, but they tell you how to add some tastiness to the packaged good. They also give of themselves; their dos and don'ts are not arbitrary but they stress that their method is one that they have arrived at through experimentation."

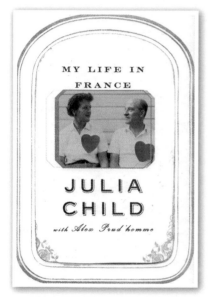

Despite Jones's praise, the head of Knopf didn't have great hopes for the book.

"Alfred Knopf, the imperious head of the publishing house, who fancied himself a gourmand, was skeptical that a big woman from Smith College and her friends could write a meaningful work on *la cuisine française*. But he was willing to give it a chance. Then, when Judith announced that we'd decided to call the book *Mastering the Art of French Cooking,* Alfred shook his head and scoffed: 'I'll eat my hat if anyone buys a book with that title!' (From Child's memoir *My Life in France*.)

"History had different plans. *Mastering the Art of French Cooking* went on to great acclaim. *The New York Times*' Craig Claiborne believed it "may be the finest volume on French cooking ever published in English."

Many believe that much of the book's success coincided with Child's delightful first appearance on Boston's Public TV station near her home in Cambridge. According to Biography.com:

"Displaying her trademark forthright manner and hearty humor, she prepared an omelet on air. The public's response was enthusiastic, generating 27 letters and countless phone calls—'a remarkable response,' a station executive remembered, 'given that station management occasionally wondered if 27 viewers were tuned in.' She was then invited back to tape her own series on cooking for the network, initially earning $50 a show (it was later raised to $200, plus expenses)."

And though the PBS shows made her a household name, it's worth repeating that a major part of her reputation stemmed from her rigorous devotion to getting recipes exactly right. As her *New York Times* obituary stated, "When she wrote recipes, they were long and detailed because, she said, she felt obligated to ensure their success. 'A cookbook is only as good as its worst recipe,' she said. All ten of her cookbooks were held up as models of clarity. She was also adamant that cooking was not like free-form jazz: she intended her recipes to be followed to the letter."

And her recipes could be trusted because of her extremely high standards. In her memoir *My Life in France*, Child explained her detailed process.

> "I subjected every recipe to what we called 'the operational proof': that is, it's all theory until you see for yourself whether or not something works," she wrote.

> "Working on soups, for instance, I made a soup a day chez Child...I consulted Simca's recipe as well as the established recipes of Montagne, Larousse, Ali-Bab and Curnonsky. I read through all of them, then made the soup three different ways—following two recipes exactly as written, and making one adaptation for the pressure cooker...At dinner, my guinea pig, Paul complimented the three soups aux choux but I wasn't satisfied. One of the secrets to make this dish work, I felt, was to make a vegetable-and-ham stock before the cabbage was put in; also, not to cook the cabbage too long, which gives it a sour taste. But should the cabbage be blanched? Should I use a different variety of cabbage? Would the pressure-cooked soup taste better if I used the infernal machine a shorter time? I had to iron out all these questions."

No wonder *The New York Times* obituary went on to say:

> "What made Mrs. Child such an influential teacher was her good-humored insistence that competent home cooks, if they followed instructions, would find even complicated French dishes within their grasp. Mistakes were not the end of the world, just part of the game.

> In fact, minor slips and mishaps were weekly events on 'The French Chef,' and none of them seemed to faze Mrs. Child. At the same time, she always put the food before showmanship. She had real respect for recipes, and by example she helped elevate the status of cooking in the United States."

Judith Jones told *The Boston Globe* in 2009, "Julia really changed the way we wrote cookbooks. She changed expectations of what a cookbook should be... She made people see that cooking was fun and sensual. She made sounds that were delicious. She lifted the hideous Puritanism that had, particularly in New England, made food uninteresting...She adapted to what we have in America and found substitutes. You didn't have to go to 10 markets looking for a shallot; if it wasn't there, it wasn't there....And she would have said 'nonsense' to what's going on today when they call for one sprig of fresh parsley, three fresh bay leaves...You spend about $9 on what's practically a decoration."

It's that no-nonsense practicality—combined with witty showmanship—that made Child such a beloved figure in the culinary world. Her rules were charming and really worked.

And one of her golden rules in the kitchen remains one of my favorite mottos in life. Mind you, I think it can be applied to the art of writing a cookbook as well.

Words of Wisdom

T. Susan Chang is a rare and wonderful voice in food journalism. She's not afraid to share her opinion—even if it will ruffle a few feathers. As the cookbook reviewer for *The Boston Globe* and columnist for *Eat Your Books* and a blogger (http://tsusanchang.wordpress.com/), she has reviewed hundreds of cookbooks—and chosen NOT to review thousands more. She's followed the evolution of cookbook publishing and has more than a few helpful thoughts on everything from recipe testing to art direction, and the blog-to-book phenomenon. She has generously offered to share her thoughts with us as long as I agreed to run them by her first. She's decided that she's racked up enough enemies from her reviews—she'd prefer not to add any more to the list when she's trying to be helpful. Below are some of Susan's most helpful hints:

➪ Among other things, I think the explosion of the blog-to-book industry has had an impact on publishing that is really indicative of the strengths and weaknesses of the industry. On the strengths side, visuals get better and better every year. When the design of a book is great, the books are easier to use. But on the flip side, there is still quite a bit of sucking up content that is already out there in blog form and putting it into a book—as another merchandising opportunity. I think bloggers should create original material for a hard copy book. They need to make the book separate and stand on its own from the blog.

➪ I feel like there needs to be a comprehensive solution to the recipe testing problem. It's really gotten to the point where there are authors you trust and ones you don't. Those are the authors who send the recipes out to all of their friends, cross-test and test with many different levels of cooks. Although many publishers say you have to test, there is no real industry standard, so that recipes get short shrift. I'm hearing that the budget, if there's much of a budget at all, is going to go to pictures. But remember, if the cookbook is going to last, the recipes have to work.

➠ When I am deciding whether to review, basically I'm looking for three things first of all: newness, usefulness and thoughtfulness. I hate to see the same recipes over and over, somebody trying to tell me that their take is unique. I look for books that I can cook from for a week straight—normal meals, lunches, breakfasts and dinners and then get maybe 12 recipes I feel good about, and ones that I want to cook over and over. As for thoughtfulness, I like the author who goes the extra distance in the headnotes and instruction. He shows me where to find a difficult ingredient, what to substitute, what weird thing that you think might have gone wrong, and offers sensory cues that are not the obvious ones.

➠ If the books pass my first three hurdles, then I go for charm. I am a big sucker for beautiful books and good stories. Of course I have some favorite cookbook writers: Raghavan Iyer, Martha Holmberg, Susie Middleton, Dorie Greenspan. I find them pretty consistent. I like David Tanis, Molly Stephens, Fuchsia Dunlop, although *Every Grain of Rice* a little overhyped, I like Roy Finamore, some of Melissa Clark's books, Issa Chandra Moskowitz, Louisa Shafia, Marcella's *Essentials of Classic Italian Cooking*. I love Claudia Roden, but not as crazy about Paula Wolfert. I have mixed opinions about Alice Waters—her books are not the most usable. I love the way she thinks, feels and communicates about food, and have recommended the *Art of Simple Food* to innumerable new cooks. I love her sensibility, but I don't know that she makes the hugest contribution. There's this problem: What if you don't have access to a farmers' market near Berkeley, or beautiful fresh sorrel?

There is no right way to write a recipe, but there are plenty of wrong ones, so be diligent, get lots of readers and cross-testers. You need to make sure that your reader (and cook in his or her kitchen) will never be left hanging. The hanging quickly turns into bad results and bad results turn into bad reviews and bad reviews kill sales. Bottom line: If you want your book to sell well, write a good recipe.

Chapter 6

More Words—What Else Do You Need to Include?

A good cookbook should also be more than the sum of its collection of recipes. The best ones can also be reference guides. They teach people as much as possible about the subject matter—whether it's a single technique, a specific country's cuisine or every nitty-gritty thing you learned from competing on a hit reality show. They can also inspire readers to be more authoritative and creative in the kitchen. So the more insight you can share, the better off the reader will be.

Like my publisher and guru Will Kiester says, "A good book isn't good for one reason, it's good for 20 different reasons."

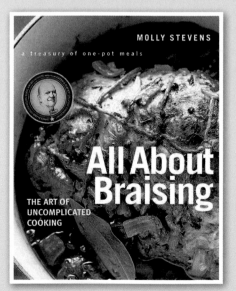

"The books that have gravitas and last in value have a carefully thought out, developed philosophy behind them," adds Molly Stevens, who cowrote *One Potato, Two Potato* and wrote *All About Braising*.

Fortunately, there are different ways to achieve this goal. You can also feel free to mix more than one of the styles below. When it comes to the non-recipe section of a cookbook, feel free to experiment a little.

"I don't think there are fundamentals that every cookbook should have," says Stevens. "But each should have a reason for existing...something that makes it indispensable. When people tell me they want to write a cookbook....well, have something to say."

If you can, try and write—or at least outline—what you would like to accomplish in the introduction and chapter (or chapters) leading up to the recipe section.

Stevens admits that's a goal she rarely achieves. "I usually write after I've done the recipes and headnotes and I think there's a bad reason for it," she admits. "It would be better to do it as I go but it looms over me. I worry about it because it feels so important. I want it to match what's in the book—so it's kind of like the cart and horse thing—which comes first?"

A Cookbook Intro That Teaches

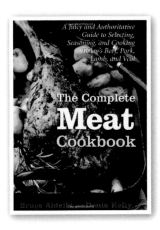

Many cookbook authors have found success by focusing on one technique or ingredient. If that's the case, then think of the front of this type of book as being a culinary encyclopedia of ideas about the subject matter. It should be packed with facts—some basic, some harder-won insight that you've gleaned from your personal observations from all your time in the kitchen.

Stevens is a great example of someone who does this in her books. "When I am writing, I just try to imagine myself in the kitchen. I'm pantomiming through the steps in my brain. That's my whole approach...when I am writing, I am trying to teach....It's my natural tendency to put in as much information because I want to teach how to do it. I want it to be like I was standing in the kitchen with you."

Another good teacher is Bruce Aidells, who wrote *The Complete Meat Cookbook*: *A Juicy and Authoritative Guide to Selecting, Seasoning, and Cooking Today's Beef, Pork, Lamb, and Veal* (Houghton Mifflin, © 1998) Before he even gets to his first recipe he includes 75 pages of detailed material that, among other things, tells the reader how to use the book, refrigerate beef and recommends what other ingredients to use. (For instance, he prefers using homemade stock but urges readers to go light with the salt if using canned stocks "as some become quite salty if reduced to make a sauce.")

A Cookbook Intro That Preaches

Other cookbooks are beloved because they succeed in getting you to think differently about how to shop, cook or spend time in the kitchen. In that case, use your introduction to wax eloquently about a philosophical idea or cause célèbre. Argue your case for buying only organic ingredients or eating a plant-based diet.

Stevens says one of her favorite cookbook writers in this category is Hugh Fearnley-Whittingstall. "I really admire people who can be preachy. I love the passion he has when he writes about food and ingredients."

A good example of the soapbox comes from his latest cookbook, *River Cottage Light & Easy*, published by Bloomsbury in September 2014. It comes in the introduction, where he writes:

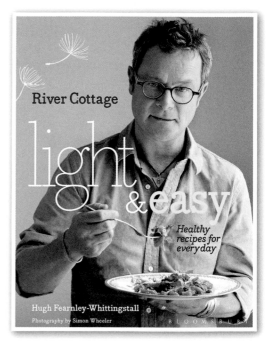

> "Exploring and extolling the life-enhancing effects of cooking and eating great food is what I do. And I'm increasingly convinced of a couple of things. Really delicious, satisfying food doesn't have to be time-consuming and complicated. And it certainly needn't be rich and laden with fat. What's more, healthy food doesn't have to be ascetic, restrictive or centered on denial.
>
> Lovely and exciting as good meat and fish are to cook with, they make us lazy in the kitchen. Put them on one side—for a while, or for a few days a week—and a torrent of vegetable creativity will be released. I want to encourage a change in your cooking—and the phrase 'light and easy' gets pretty much to the heart of the matter.
>
> Underpinning my idea of 'light' is a notion that may raise a few eyebrows. I want to address the suspect ubiquity of a couple of very familiar ingredients. They are milk and wheat. My goodness, they are everywhere! My question is, do they deserve to be quite so popular? Are they that good for us, that indispensable, that we must all consume them by the kilo, week in, week out? I've been thinking about this, and exploring alternatives, and I'm convinced the answer is a resounding no! We need to recognize that wheat and dairy products can be problematic for many of us—and, in excess, perhaps for most of us.
>
> Dairy ingredients can also be a challenge to human digestive systems. It is widely recognized that at least 70 per cent of the world's adult population produce low levels of lactase, the enzyme needed to break down the milk sugar lactose. Digestive problems caused by dairy ingredients are a problem everywhere. I bet most of us know someone who struggles with them. And of course there is no question that cream, butter and many cheeses are high in the saturated fats that can contribute to rising cholesterol levels.
>
> The science of diet is complex and remains controversial—especially around wheat and dairy products. Personal testimony often cuts compellingly through the heated 'scientific' debate. Perhaps, like me, you know people whose bodies and lives were in turmoil until it was suggested they try giving up wheat. If so, you will know just how rapid and complete a recovery can follow this simple change of habit."

Bestselling American author Barbara Kafka is one of America's most storied preachers (although many would characterize her style with a little less flattery). In the introduction to the innovative and groundbreaking *Roasting: A Simple Art*, Kafka opines about how cooking has evolved over the years. (It's important to note that I worked on this book when it was published. It was my first "big book" and I had no idea how heated [pardon the pun] the high-heat cooking debate could get. Full pages in newspaper sections across the country were devoted to the debate: should I roast my chicken at 500 degrees and fill the house with smoke [Barbara actually recommended you unhook your smoke detectors in her interview] or should you go low and slow?)

> "It seems to me that less cooking is done today than used to be and that when it is done, it is so much more work because we have lost the habit of continuous cooking. We start each meal from scratch with fresh shopping and a brand-new independent recipe. Our predecessors didn't, and we can save ourselves a great deal of work, and have better, more economical food with greater depth of flavor by seeing cooking as an ongoing process. There is no better way to get in the habit than with roast birds, meats and fish."

Sing it, Sister Barbara.

A Cookbook Intro That Tells Your Personal Story

People want to know who you are. In today's world, revealing personal details about your life is more important than ever. That doesn't mean printing your resume in the pages of your cookbook. Tell readers what your mom used to cook for you, how you first got into cooking and when you really fell in love with it. Tell them why you decided you just had to write a book about your time in (fill in name of country) or opening that nationally acclaimed gastropub.

In her cookbook *A Girl and Her Pig*, April Bloomfield, the chef behind The Spotted Pig, The Breslin Bar & Dining Room, The John Dory Oyster Bar and Salvation Taco in New York City and Tosca Café in San Francisco, writes about how she dreamed of being a cop but settled for cooking school because she liked the uniform. And she eloquently describes how she still loves being in the kitchen after years and years.

> "Even after all this time in the kitchen, I still love watching garlic go nutty in hot fat or peeking underneath a piece of caramelizing fennel to see it browning and growing sweeter by the minute. I love spooning pan liquid over roasting meat, piling any vegetable matter on top and gently smooshing it. And as many livers as I've seared in my life, the smell of one meeting a hot pan still makes my knees tremble."

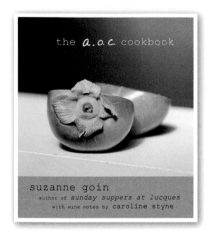

Don't Forget to Include All Your Kitchen Nuggets of Information

If you're a successful chef, you have spent an enormous amount of brainpower observing the little details in the kitchen. As Suzanne Goin says in her introduction to *The A.O.C Cookbook*, "Learning to cook really is just like learning another language. You have to do it rigorously, practice, and pay attention. Every time you cook, it is a chance to learn and take away a lesson."

If you're writing a cookbook, it's your job to be a good translator. Figure out what particular insights you have learned and be sure to share them with your reader. Let them learn from your mistakes in the kitchen. Chances are you have 100 of these insights a day but don't realize it. Below are a few of my favorite examples:

- Barbara Kafka on the importance of knowing every oven is not the same: "Getting to know an oven is much like adjusting to the quirks in a cranky automobile or a friend and just as vital for happiness."

- Molly Stevens on avoiding burning yourself when using a foil lid while braising food: "Somehow a foil lid seems to release steam in a more malevolent fashion than a regular lid."

- Mario Batali on how much pasta to cook for each person at a party: "I recommend serving about 2 ounces of dried pasta per person as a first course in a three-course meal, and about 4 ounces for a main course."

- J.M. Hirsch on some surprising ways to use hot sauce in *High Flavor, Low Labor*: "This is my secret ingredient in hummus and cheese sauces. Just a dash brightens the other flavors without adding significant heat. Try it in macaroni and cheese or mixed into burgers. Use it to perk up mayonnaise for a sandwich or potato salad. Also try it in a vinaigrette or a hearty salad (something with meat and cheese in it)."

The lesson here? Pay attention to every little detail that goes on during the cooking process and write it down. And share your quirks and obsessions with the reader. Barbara Kafka was brilliant at that. In her *Soups: A Way of Life* book, she writes, "In recent years I have become addicted to Japanese wooden lids, otoshi-buta, when making stock. They come in sets with wooden handles. They are meant to fit inside a pot, leaving about a half inch all around them. This keeps the stock or other liquid from reducing too much as it simmers. It also helps to keep the solids under the liquid, where they belong." That's helpful and a piece of equipment I would certainly like because my stocks never taste very good.

Words of Wisdom

Molly Stevens isn't just one of T. Susan Chang's favorite authors, but one of mine, too. I was also lucky enough to meet her as a young publicist (and cook from her books). Her book, *All About Braising*, became almost obsessional for me, and not just because I was dying to buy my first piece of Le Creuset. Her recipes were so detailed and interesting, I could picture myself in the kitchen as I was reading them. Below she shares her writing tips. Writing for most cookbook authors is much more difficult than cooking. After all, if you're accomplished enough to consider writing a book, then you're probably a pretty good cook. Writing is also a skill that takes years to perfect. Here are some suggestions to shorten that timeline.

» Figure out if you have the chops to write. "Start small. Try to write a few things down and have someone look at them. You'll find out quickly whether or not you have the aptitude and sensibility of a writer. Sitting down and typing this stuff out is tedious for a lot of people. But if that's not your strength it doesn't mean you can't write a book, it means it might be hard to go it alone. Vice versa, if you have a gift as a writer and enjoy it, but the ideas and inspiration aren't there, work with someone who is brilliant in the kitchen but can't transpose that."

» Tune others out: "For me and a lot of writers, the biggest challenge is to hear your own voice as your writing as opposed to thinking about what it's going to look like out there and how people will respond to it. It's very difficult to write authentically if you are already hearing the critics, bloggers and reviewers. If you can somehow cancel that noise and figure out what it is you have to say about something, not what everybody else is saying."

» Limit procrastination: "Keep your ass in the chair. You've just got to keep writing. There are definitely moments when I feel in the zone but sometimes I am literally banging my head against the desk. Just keep at it. It's the most clichéd thing in the world but write it one word at a time. If you have to, take a walk, go back to the kitchen or do some push-ups. But if you do that all the time, you will not get this done....at some point you have to stay in the chair."

» Do not be afraid if your book changes as you are developing it. Make room in your brain for that. Examine that. Maybe you need to get back on track and your book should stay what it was or maybe your book should be something else, too. Even if you have a short deadline, don't panic. Remember, it's your book. So make it your book.

» Molly also gives a good index. About this afterthought for most she says, "Things should be listed in a logical but also diverse way. For example, is hamburger just under hamburger or just brown beef? You know, cross-referencing instead of just recipe titles."

In many books, equipment or technique books for example, information can get very repetitive. If you're steaming, how many recipes do you really need? Wouldn't a chart be more helpful? When thinking about additional material to include, also think about the best way to represent it. Maybe a chart or graph, or a step-by-step photo will do the job of 10,000 words. And that brings us to the Art Program, aka, the place where all cookbook advances go to die.

Chapter 7

The Art Program

∿∿∿

Cookbooks need to look good—chock-full of gorgeous four-color photos and an engaging, easy-to-follow design. At one time I would have said that there is absolutely no way to publish a cookbook without hiring a team. Your team would include a photographer, food stylist and prop stylist. This team would interpret your vision (and your recipes) and capture them for the page. It's not so black-and-white anymore. Even Susan Spungen, one of the world's best food stylists and a personal hero (I had her cakes that she developed for *Martha Stewart Living* when she was the food editor there in the nineties as the design motif for my wedding!) told me that more and more people, especially bloggers, are shooting their own books and they are good enough. Are they as good as a professional team? Probably not; but they are intimate and approachable and probably exactly what the reader expects from their beloved blogger.

This chapter will not teach you how to be a graphic designer, photographer or food stylist. These professionals spend years honing their crafts and it's offensive to think that any person with an iPhone can be a great food photographer overnight or that any chef that knows how to plate food will make a good picture. However, there are many lessons you can learn that will help you make your book as visually compelling as it is as a read—again, a critical piece on your road to a bestseller.

Spend any time in the cookbook section of the bookstore and you will soon realize that cookbooks come in many shapes and sizes. From big, beautiful coffee-table books to small, gifty single-subject books and everything in between, the choices in a cookbook package can be overwhelming.

Your publisher will guide the design process but you should offer an informed opinion. Since only the very rare cookbook now isn't four-color throughout with photographs illustrating practically every recipe, we're going to assume your book will be rich in pictures. Now that that's out of the way, you need to decide what the house for all of these photos and recipes is going to look like. That "house" is what's known in the trade as the package.

The book package includes everything that makes up the physical book, including trim size, jacket treatment, case, paper specification, binding and type and color of ink. Publishers become known for a certain type of package. Artisan Books, a division of Workman Publishing, specializes in coffee-table books. Its books are as famous for their designs as they are for their authors. The bestselling *French Laundry Cookbook,* written by Thomas Keller and photographed by Deborah Jones, was published in 1999 and set a new standard in cookbook design. Measuring 11.3 x 11.3 inches and more than an inch thick, *The French Laundry Cookbook* was designed by Level Inc. from Calistoga, California, and went on to win an International Association of Culinary Professionals award for Best Design. Workman Publishing, Artisan's parent company, made its reputation (and sales) almost exclusively because of its book designs. Exclusively paperback, the Workman Cookbooks

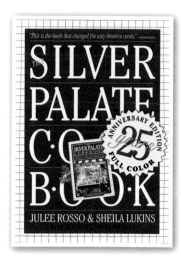
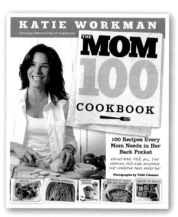

(the mega bestselling *The Silver Palate Cookbook* being one of the first) are known for very information-dense layouts inspired by magazine publishers, with large amounts of illustrations and a heavy reliance on sidebars to convey information not directly stated in the text itself. If you sell a cookbook to Workman, you will have a good idea what your book will look like as its signature design varies little. Page Street Publishing has also established a signature look—original trade paperbacks with rich color photographs and energetic type treatments, most priced under $25.

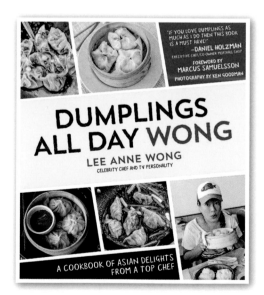

Deciding the best look for your book comes from your content and your publisher. *Dumplings All Day Wong* (Page Street, August 2014), by Lee Anne Wong, for example, is a fun book. Described as "a cookbook of Asian delights from a top chef" and with a pun in the title, it would be hard to mistake this as a book that should be oversized and cost more than $25, even though it's written by a very experienced and acclaimed chef. The subject is dumplings and Wong's tone in the writing is accessible and meant to encourage having fun in the kitchen—and the look of the book matches exactly that.

Words of Wisdom

How do you and your publisher find such a good match? We again consulted our oracle, Pam Krauss.

▶ We like to solicit opinions from our authors on the design. While we certainly don't expect them to know which particular fonts they like or how many picas of white space they want after the yield of the recipe, we give the authors a great deal of freedom to select their photographer and with most of the books we publish, the photographs set the tone for the design. The size of the book, the binding, the paper choice— all of those decisions come from the photographs.

▶ And then we run the numbers to make sure the intended design and the target audience match. Is this a book that will be used mostly in the kitchen or is it a trophy book? If it's a trophy book, we're not as concerned with readability but really concerned about how the photographs will print on the paper.

▶ When we're making books that we know people are going to regularly cook from we are much more pragmatic. We want to make sure that when the book is laid flat the reader can take in the whole recipe at one glance. We make sure recipes are broken up in digestible chunks so you can come back and find your place after you sauté the onions.

▶ Ina Garten's books are a great example of really kitchen-friendly books (that look pretty good too, of course). The type is very straightforward and large, the books are made with a lay-flat binding and you really feel at home as soon as you open it. It's not always necessary to completely reinvent the wheel—in Ina's package, we've created a recognizable brand that fits her aesthetic and delivers what her readers want—a book that works in and out of the kitchen.

▶ A book that is out now that is a really good example of the photography, typography and author's voice really working well is *Thug Kitchen* (Rodale, October 2014). The authors shot their photos, and while it's not necessarily Quentin Bacon or David Loftus photography, they are perfectly respectable author photos. They wouldn't have worked on glossy paper—but printed on matte, they look just fine. Perfect even.

Food Photography

We all have our favorite food photographers—especially cookbook authors. Jamie Oliver uses David Loftus. Ina Garten works with Quentin Bacon. Award-winning author and photographer Naomi Duguid uses Gentl & Hyers for the non-location food photography. Thomas Keller works with Deborah Jones. How do you find your David Loftus?

Once again, go back to the books you love (and magazines and Instagram!) and put together a list of all of the photographers you like and start looking at their portfolios online. Once you choose the photographer, that will set the tone for the entire book, so make sure you're happy with your choice. Also make sure you can afford the photographer's fee. Marquee names like the ones above can cost as much as $100,000 to shoot a book, but most, and especially the up-and-comers, will do a book for $10,000 and under, because a book is

(continued)

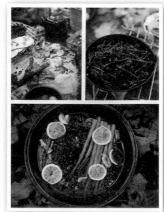

a prestigious calling card. Every day, new photographers are coming into the marketplace and most of them are dying to shoot a cookbook. For a freelance photographer, it's a great gig, and an important piece of work to add to the portfolio. So get creative when thinking about how to finance your photography.

Spotlight: Food Styling

Australian food blogger, photographer and founder of the Virtual Cooking School, Jules Clancy of stonesoup.com posted her "10 Tips to Improve Your Food Photography" on www.digitalfoodphotography.school.com and we think they are spot on:

1. Use less food than you normally would
While it may seem more generous to serve plates piled high with food, an overcrowded plate can look less appealing than a minimalist spread. Think about how you can use the white space of the plate to frame your dish.

2. Use paper to add texture to plates
Lining plates with parchment or baking paper helps to add visual interest and soften the lines of your plates.

3. Look for contrast with backgrounds
While there are times when all white on white can be visually striking, I find I get better shots if I go for contrast. So a pale-colored food and plate gets a dark background, whereas a vibrantly colored dish tends to be best with a simple white background.

4. Allow food to spill over naturally
Getting a bit messy really helps to add movement and life to your photographs, rather than having everything confined to plates and bowls.

5. Choose simple crockery and tableware
While highly decorative China and linens are beautiful on their own, they can detract from the visual impact of the food. Plain plates, especially classic white, allow the food to be the star.

6. Emphasize the natural beauty of the food
Try and think about what it is that makes a particular dish look delicious and then serve it in a way to flaunt it. For example, I love the golden, crispy skin of a well-roasted chicken. Rather than carve the chicken into individual slices with tiny slivers of skin visible, the whole bird tends to look best.

(continued)

7. Get some work-in-progress shots

It can be easy to focus on getting the final plated-up food shot and miss out on some great opportunities along the way. Try taking a few shots during the preparation and cooking process.

8. Try and capture the "yum" factor

Think about what makes your subject really delicious and then aim to highlight this characteristic in your shot. Ice cream is a great example. It's all about smooth creaminess and licking drips from the sides of your cone or bowl.

9. Always be on the lookout for ideas

Inspiration can strike from anywhere. When you're eating out or even just flicking through your favorite food magazine, take note of what looks appealing and what doesn't.

10. Dig in and reshoot

Once you have a shot of the whole dish that you love, eat or serve some out and then take another shot. Often a half-finished plate is more appetizing than the original whole.

Cover Design

Unless you are a very, VERY big star, the focus of your book cover should be a great food photograph. Check out a selection of some of my favorite jackets:

THE FRENCH LAUNDRY COOKBOOK
THOMAS KELLER

PLENTY
Vibrant Vegetable Recipes from London's Ottolenghi

YOTAM OTTOLENGHI

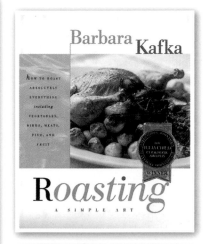

Barbara Kafka

HOW TO ROAST ABSOLUTELY EVERYTHING including VEGETABLES, BIRDS, MEATS, FISH, AND FRUIT

Roasting
A SIMPLE ART

PRUNE

BLOOD, BONES & BUTTER

gabrielle hamilton

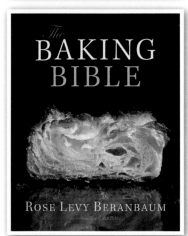

The
BAKING
BIBLE

ROSE LEVY BERANBAUM
The Cake Bible

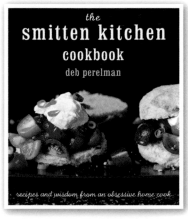

the
smitten kitchen
cookbook
deb perelman

recipes and wisdom from an obsessive home cook

light on calories, big on flavor
the skinnytaste cookbook
GINA HOMOLKA
with Heather K. Jones, R.D.

BAKING
CHEZ MOI
Recipes from My Paris Home to Your Home Anywhere

DORIE GREENSPAN

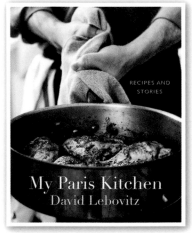

RECIPES AND
STORIES

My Paris Kitchen
David Lebovitz

Words of Wisdom:
Susan Spungen

Just back from teaching food styling at a creative retreat hosted by blogger Modern Farmette called Lens & Larder (http://farmette.ie/2014/08/14/lens-larder/), Susan was full of new media info to share—which was hilarious and ironic to me because I had called to interview her about her food styling craft. Susan is widely considered one of the best food stylists in the world. She was the first food editor at *Martha Stewart Living*, and cooked and baked and styled more food than any of us could imagine. After that she began writing her own cookbooks and styling food for films, most notably *Julie & Julia* directed by the late, brilliant Nora Ephron. She's a devoted Instagrammer (and even met Modern Farmette) through the platform and our conversation covered a lot of ground. Here are some of the highlights:

➤ I'm not surprised that publishers are allowing bloggers to shoot their own books. Most of the pictures are good enough. One recent and notable exception is the bestselling *Skinnytaste Cookbook* by Gina Homolka. I worked on that and Gina was very clear that her photos weren't good enough for Clarkson Potter and she was thrilled to have a team around her. The book is gorgeous and both the author and publisher love it.

➤ I am still trying to wrap my head around professional food stylists and blogger food stylists and the fauxtographers. If a person takes really great pictures on Instagram, why not hire them to do a book? Is it a different product? Sure. Is it good enough? Sure. I shot my *Hostess* book myself. They were small pictures and very how-to. I had to be fast and dirty. You don't want to go broke doing your book. But don't be greedy, either. If they give you a big advance, hire a team.

➤ I'm trying to change with the times because I think our economy is dictating a lot right now. Bloggers have been getting much bigger advances and selling more books than me. Does that make me sad? Sure, but what does it teach me? I need to build my social media platform, and my skills are perfect for Instagram. I just think to survive in any world, in any business at this time, you have to be adaptable. The people who want to do things the way things have always been done can really fall behind. When I think about the history, these big bloggers (Made with Cinnamon is 18!) were small children when *Martha Stewart Living* started and don't care. It's not about magazines anymore. Pinterest and Instagram are where things are happening.

➤ Don't expect you can do it all yourself if you have to shoot all of your recipes in four days. Maybe you want to shoot them yourself, and then hire a food stylist. If you have no idea what you're doing, then hire the whole team. It can be really expensive, but in this climate, top people will work at reduced rates because it's a chance to be more creative, because they are creating a beautiful product. And content is still king.

▶ I love where food styling and food photography are right now. They're immediate and not fussy. Food looks best when it's fresh and when you can see what it is. Overhead is a really big angle currently, because it's in your face, and in many cases it's the best angle to shoot the food. Of course it's popular on social media because it's also the easiest way to shoot the food.

▶ What are the important things I look for in a good food picture? I was just looking at *Plenty More* by Yotam Ottolenghi. It's exciting. The pictures made me want to make the recipes, which is number one. It's hard to articulate, but you want the reader to be struck by the excitement of making the recipes. The pictures should look exciting and delicious. Ottolenghi's food is inherently and naturally beautiful. I like to point to "form and freshness" as the two most important things. You need to articulate the shapes of the food, so you can identify everything immediately even if it's an unfamiliar dish. And color of course. Hopefully no one is making food that is brown and ugly and boring. Try to find a way to make the recipes more interesting and colorful, and if you're not shooting every recipe, choose the ones that are most exciting and beautiful.

▶ As a stylist and a recipe writer, I literally try to put myself in the shoes of the cook. In a cookbook you have the luxury of more space for tips and extras. A book is a place to make sure the reader understands how to make the recipe. I try to not leave anyone there scratching his head. You need to address those things and remember what it's like to not know how to cook. We have the luxury of the photographs—make sure they tell you everything you need to know that you won't see in the recipe.

▶ Food stylists are the best recipe testers you can get. If they make your recipe following your directions, and it doesn't look anything like your dish, then there is a problem with the recipe. The investment in your food stylist doubles as an investment in recipe testing. You really get two for the price of one.

Word of Wisdom:
Susi Oberhelman

Susi Oberhelman is an art director who has designed hundreds of cookbooks. She was the art director at Artisan Books when I worked there, and has since started her own company (SVO Graphic Design). She has some pretty clear thoughts about "good design" that will help guide you through the process.

➡ Whenever I go to start a design for a recipe, I want to pick out the ingredients easy and fast so I list them cleanly and put them to the side of the recipe so they have room to breathe. And then I make sure the method has enough space to be able to read. I'm really going for readability.

➡ To get good readability, you need to consider size, as in the letters need to be big enough to read. As beautiful as the Thomas Keller cookbooks are, I find them hard to follow. The ingredients are tucked away, the columns don't align or they center them. Design the recipes for the reader, not for your portfolio.

➡ I try to fit the mood of the book or what the subject matter should feel like. In *Good to the Grain*, all of the photography was dark and moody so the book needed a slab serif font to go with the photography—nothing too feminine.

Susi went on to caution that while good design is most definitely subjective, it's important to always be thinking of your reader, which must be good advice, because in every chapter, in every part of the book, every person interviewed talked about how you needed to be in service to your reader.

PART THREE

Selling Out

Chapter 8

The Social Media Revolution

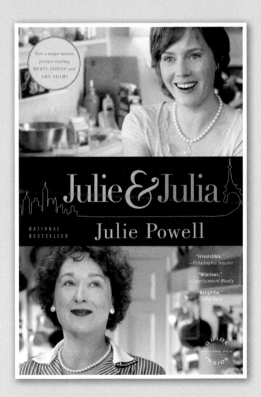

By now, you're familiar with the modern fairy tale in which a plucky girl or guy finds fame and fortune with a simple blog post. Yes, the Internet has truly become an indispensable tool for making a name for yourself. In fact, you virtually have no shot at a publishing career now without using social media somehow—which means using it well and constantly.

In the world of food blogging, it all began with Julie Powell. In 2002, the 29-year-old Long Island City resident was bored with her secretarial job at the Lower Manhattan Development Corporation, so she started The Julie/Julia Project, a series of blog posts on Salon.com about trying to cook every dish from Julia Child's book *Mastering the Art of French Cooking* in one year. While Child didn't consider Powell a serious cook (and was pretty vocal about this woman trying to steal her thunder), thousands of people fell for her blunt and funny attempts to make sense of French cooking techniques—as well as her aimless life. (It was as if Bridget Jones had decided to attend—and swear profusely about her adventures—Le Cordon Bleu.) Just before the yearlong project ended, Powell told *The New York Times* "by making my life crazier, [the blog] gave me structure it was lacking. It assuages my helplessness." It also gave her a book deal from Little, Brown & Company and a movie based on the book starring Amy Adams and Meryl Streep. Powell ultimately decided that she was more into writing than cooking but her blog still paved the way for many others to establish themselves as breakout stars in the industry.

In 2004, television executive Lisa Lillien began turning her personal 30-pound weight loss tale into an incredibly successful diet and nutrition brand. She used $10,000 of her own savings to launch *Hungry Girl*, a website and daily e-newsletter that detailed her journey finding and cooking tasty dishes that were also calorie conscious. What began as a daily e-newsletter to 200 friends and family members became a media empire with over one million subscribers. In 2010, Lillien received an advance of more than $10 million for eight books (six out of the nine she's written so far have debuted at number one on *The New York Times* "Advice, How-To and Miscellaneous" bestseller list). She also writes online columns for *Weight Watchers* and *People* magazines and stars in television shows on the Cooking Channel and the Food Network.

Lillien credits her brand's phenomenal rise to two simple factors. She offered people something different from the usual diet advice—and she did it regularly. "Hungry Girl is unique because it's fun and funny—a rarity for diet and nutrition content," she told *Good Housekeeping.com*. "It's also unique because I offer different information every day. It's important to set yourself apart from the rest." Fans also craved her no-nonsense, BFF tone. "She doesn't preach or talk down to anybody, and believe me, that is not always true when it comes to women my size," explained Stephanie Brown, a self-described plus-sized woman who spoke to *The New York Times* when she attended a cocktail party and book signing for Lillien's 2010 book *Hungry Girl Happy Hour*.

In May 2006, Ree Drummond's signature voice and an incredibly romantic story staked her claim in the blogosphere. *ThePioneerWoman.com* recounts tales from her life on a cattle ranch near Pawhuska, Oklahoma. As she says on her site, "I met and fell in love with a rugged cowboy. Now I live in the middle of nowhere on a working cattle ranch. My days are spent wrangling children, chipping dried manure from boots, washing jeans, and making gravy...here I write daily about my long transition from spoiled girl to domestic country wife."

Then slice up half of the onion.

Cut three or four Roma tomatoes in half lengthwise.

Make three or four slices...

Then slice in the other direction to create a dice.

The recipe portion of her site came a year later when she wrote a detailed post on how to cook a steak. Readers loved it and wanted more, so Drummond began sharing her recipes, along with detailed step-by-step photos. "Her cooking strikes a chord with lots of people in this country who are interested in feeding their families better food without getting into molecular gastronomy," Bobby Flay told *The New Yorker* in 2007. When Drummond launched a contest asking her readers to submit their favorite home recipe, the response—more than 5,000 submissions in less than 24 hours!—convinced her there was a real desire for simple but home-cooked meals.

Drummond's award-winning blog—and beloved recipes—helped make her the newest gem in the Food Network's jewel box. According to a *Wall Street Journal* article in 2013, her show is the most watched show with 25 to 54-year-old women, the audience most coveted by advertisers. "Many watch because they want to appreciate a beautiful lifestyle they don't have," the Food Network's General Manager Bob Tuschman told the *Journal*. That desire to live vicariously also helped Drummond snag three cookbook deals—and three bestsellers. (She has also published three children's books and a memoir that Reese Witherspoon has been mentioned to star in an upcoming film version.)

But before you start dream casting who would play you in the film version of your life, let's figure out how you can find success in a world that's frankly oversaturated with blogs, especially if you don't live somewhere particularly exotic or know the least bit about making a meal diet-friendly or take terrible pictures. Ree—and many other generous bloggers—offer tips on their sites about creating successful blogs, so be sure to check out the advice of some of your favorites. Below are some standouts.

Spotlight:
10 Important Things I've Learned About Blogging, Posted by Ree Drummond (Aug. 8, 2010)

1. Be yourself.

Write in your own voice.

Write as if you're talking to your sister.

Unless you don't get along with your sister.

Or don't have a sister.

2. Blog often.

Whether you write a 16-paragraph essay about the cosmic implications of a free market system, a one-paragraph description of what happens to your soul when you walk into your godforsaken laundry room, or a simple photo and caption, consider your blog a precious bloom that requires daily nurturing. And watering. If you water a plant once every two weeks, it will shrivel. Unless the plant is a cactus, and then it would thrive. And to tell you the truth, I really can't figure out how a cactus fits into this analogy, so forget I brought it up.

3. Be varied.

Change things up.

Offer a smorgasbord of content.

Unless you're, say, a fashion blog.

And in that case, you should probably continue to blog about fashion.

But never blog about the same top twice!

4. Exercise more.

Blogging is an insidiously sedentary activity, and if you blog daily you should take steps to markedly increase your daily movement.

Unless that movement involves eating coffee ice cream.

In which case it would be better not to markedly increase your daily movement.

5. Allow your boundaries to set themselves naturally.

Don't feel like you have to sit down and set rules about what you will and will not blog about from day one. Just blog, and see what feels comfortable for you.

I did that.

I've found, over time, that I tend to blog about the same things I'd talk to my sister about. I've also found, over time, that I tend not to blog about things that I wouldn't talk to my sister about.

For example, I don't blog about hanky-panky.

I also don't talk to my sister about hanky-panky. If I did, she'd cover her ears and say, "Okay, gross."

And you probably would, too.

(continued)

6. Bring back retro phrases like "hanky-panky."

But only it feels right to you.

7. Don't be afraid to embarrass yourself.

On this website, over the course of the past five years, I have burped, performed Britney Spears songs in Ethel Merman's voice, misspelled words, posted typos and talked about ways I humiliated myself as both a youngster and an adult. At times, I've wondered if maybe the burps were too much.

But they're a part of me.

At least they were...until they came out of my esophagus.

But you know what I mean.

8. Try your best to spell words correctly and use proper grammar.

You don't necessarily have to wig out about it.

But do try.

It's important.

And if one or two of your readers emails you alerting you to a typo, don't be offended. Thank them profusely and sing praises for the day they were born.

9. If you have writer's block, push them through and blog anyway.

I posted the first chapter of *Black Heels & Tractor Wheels* on a morning when I woke up with the most raging case of writer's block, I couldn't even type my name.

I was sure you'd hate it, but I posted it anyway.

I went on to write 40 plus more chapters.

What if I'd given in to writer's block and decided not to blog that day?

I would never have written my Green Acres-meets-War and Peace romance novel.

And my bottom would likely be a little less jiggly.

Please see #4 above.

10. Value every person who takes time out of their day to stop by your blog.

Tell 'em you love 'em. Regularly.

11. I love ya.

More'n my luggage.

Mean it.

P-Dub.

(Sorry. That was 11 things. Please see #1 above.)

Another popular blogger, Skinny Chef Jennifer Iserloh, posted advice from Darlene Bauer, who runs Blogboldly.com, a site that offers advice on setting up and profiting from a blog. Her tips are worth listening to as well.

1. Do not be afraid to be YOU! I do not sugarcoat. I say what I think. That's me. So on my blog, I come across as your mom, or your tough but loving best friend. If you will be true to yourself, you'll have people leave your blog. But the ones who stay will absolutely love you, trust you, connect...and ultimately buy from you.

2. Add a twist. Say you're pretty funny and you want to do a blog on divorce. Make your divorce blog humorous. Yes, you'll say what needs to be said, and offer killer content...but be funny and give a little light to a painful situation. People will remember your blog.

3. More about the "twist": Explore blogs out of your niche for ideas. If you're a coach, get off the coaching blogs and check out traveling, finance, whatever. As you're looking at these blogs, see if they're doing something fun and different that you can pull back over to your (different) niche. Like I once saw a real estate agent create his brand around his dog. It's too cute and people relate to him.

Another critical component for successful blogging is real engagement with the readers. It's actually more important than audience numbers. Most businesses (publishers, TV producers, brands looking for spokespeople) would take a smaller, devoted, loyal and engaged following than a big number of people who spend no time on your site. Even established and busy stars like Ina Garten and Mario Batali take the time to help a frantic home cook. Sally McKenney, the woman behind the blog *Sally's Baking Addiction*, says she considers connecting with her readers her number-one priority and she's right. "Responding to questions that come through my blog is very important to me," she wrote in a post. "It takes quite a bit of time but I try to check in as much as I possibly can. I also try to handle emergency recipe problem emails with grace and in a timely fashion."

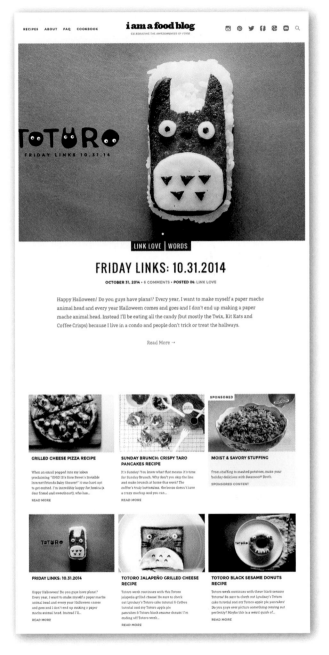

And, no surprise, the design of a blog is getting more and more sophisticated and important to attract the attention of business interests. There's a reason the latest blogger to achieve great success is Stephanie Le, whose site *I am a Food Blog* won *Saveur* magazine's "2014 Editor's Choice for Blog of the Year and Best Cooking Blog."

The editors at the culinary magazine gushed about the look of Le's work when they announced their decision.

"We found ourselves staring down at one of the most seductive pastries we've ever seen: a peach-pistachio galette that filled our monitor, larger than life. Even for people who work with food for a living, we were overcome with desire. Like so many of our favorite blogs, Le's is beautiful and inspiring. But what made hers the best of the best was its illustrative design and its lush photos, which beautifully depict foods we all want to be cooking and eating, including caviar topped latkes and Ikea-style meatballs. Le has a strong, friendly voice that segues effortlessly from explaining the importance of Bomba rice in your paella to exalting over the idea of waffled mapo tofu. Her homepage also eschews the old, reliable vertical feed in favor of a slide show with captivating fonts at the top and a clean visual grid that shows off her archive's depth below. The posts themselves are constructed with an art director's eye for composition and flow, white space and color. It's a cookbook on the computer screen, an online culinary standard-bearer."

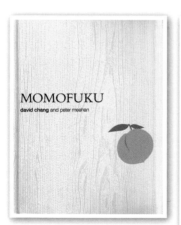

On her blog, Le explains she's come a long way since she first began blogging a la Julie Powell, when she decided to try and cook all of the recipes in the *Momofuku* cookbook. "I cringe when I look at the photos," she says. Now she shoots 98 percent in artificial light with the help of a Nikon D700 or D810 to ensure her creative dishes like *Rangoon Deviled Eggs* and *Banh Mi Tacos* look irresistible. And that dedication to detail made the Vancouver-based blogger irresistible to my comrades at Page Street Publishing, who contacted her about creating a cookbook. *Easy Gourmet: Awesome Recipes Anyone Can Cook* came out in September 2014 and quickly moved up the Amazon charts, receiving positive reviews like this one: "The straightforward recipes and gorgeous photos really deliver on the premise—showing you exactly how easy it is to make impressive meals without an excessive amount of fuss."

These success stories remind us that it's critical to: 1) find a niche, 2) be authentic about your passion and your voice, 3) continually work to develop an intimate connection with your readers, and 4) make your site stand out visually. The good news is that a standard blog isn't the only way to the promised land. Other popular forms of social media—Facebook, Twitter, Pinterest, Instagram and YouTube—can work just as well. Book publishers need evidence that you have established a real brand with potential book buyers. The smartest move is to engage in all forms of social media. The more ways you can show that masses (or fewer, but really committed fans) want to follow your every move, the more people will trust that you can sell a book—because the real dirty secret in all of this publishing business is that it will be on you to sell your book. A publisher will give you a platform, expert guidance, and if you're lucky a small budget to promote your book, but you will have to be the engine of your own success.

So where to begin? First, let's be clear. You need to build a loyal online following and then you can start selling them your cookbook. As Jeff Bullas, author of *Blogging the Smart Way* said, "you need to engage with your audience before selling anything. One rule of thumb is 80 percent of your updates should be about engagement and the other 20 percent are posts that are selling." If you jump out of the gate pushing for people to buy something, chances are you won't succeed.

Let's look at the statistics first then briefly recap how each social network can be used. Alexa Internet Inc. is a company that ranks websites based on web traffic data—i.e., page views and unique site users. Here are the results of their research as of September 2014.

#2 Facebook (Google, by the way, is number 1)
#3 YouTube
#8 Twitter
#26 Pinterest
#31 Instagram

Facebook

WHAT IT IS: The granddaddy of social media networking services has been around since 2004 and boasts about 1.32 billion users worldwide. It's the place to make new connections, stalk old pals and update people on the big and small milestones in your life. You can also share photos, links and videos.

HOW IT WORKS BEST: Get the news out about what you're doing professionally. Promote any public appearances you do as well as show photos of your recipes.

STAR CHEFS: Jamie Oliver and Anthony Bourdain both deserve nods for their use of Facebook. Oliver offers his 3 million "friends" recipes of the day and also reminds them about upcoming public appearances and effectively promotes his social initiatives with contests such as his #BetterFoodForAll lunch box challenge. Whoever sends the winning photo of how they make their kids' lunchbox better would win a free cooking class with Jamie. Bourdain weighs in on current events in the candid, cutting manner his fans love. He also promotes his CNN travel show with photos from the places he visits.

HOW IT CAN HELP SELL YOUR COOKBOOK: No doubt, Jamie Oliver helped ensure the success of his latest cookbook *Comfort Food: The Ultimate Weekend Cookbook* (Ecco, 2014) by continually previewing recipes on his site with a direct link to buy the book. He even customized the recipe ideas some days—offering Canadians specific ideas about what to use their Thanksgiving leftovers with the day after their national holiday.

Newcomer Mimi Thorisson gained selling momentum for her beautiful new book *A Kitchen in France* (Clarkson Potter, 2014) on her Facebook page. In the weeks leading up to the October 28 publication date, Thorisson, an award-winning food blogger, got the word out by offering a special giveaway—anyone who preordered the book received a stunning photograph—and previewing a brand-new recipe from the book. She also made sure to share links to any traditional media stories about her book—*In Style*, *Food52*, *Vogue* and the cover of *Conde Nast Traveler*. The result? Her book shot to number one on one of Amazon's bestseller lists before its publication date and gave Thorisson a chance to write this post: "I am chuffed and grateful...but this is also so much fun! I know this might only last for a day but it's such a great feeling. #numberonebestsellerinfrenchcooking."

Spotlight:

Understanding Facebook Engagement

To make your time on Facebook truly effective, you must get people to be active on your page, as opposed to just visiting it. Amy Porterfield, the author of *Facebook Marketing All-in-One For Dummies*, delved into the world of social media while working for motivational speaker Tony Robbins. She told Mixergy, a website that offers start-up business tips from successful entrepreneurs, that during that time she learned three key goals for every bit of content you create. "We called it Ecubing," says Porterfield. "Entertain, educate, empower. The three Es...every piece of content I create, those three words are always in the back of my mind. I think it's allowed me to be a better writer, be a better marketer."

Porterfield also offers webinars on her site AmyPorterfield.com about boosting your engagement on Facebook. It can be very helpful to take time to listen to her...check out a small part of her lectures below.

#1: Understand How Facebook Engagement Really Works

It's paramount that you understand how things *actually work* on Facebook. When you increase engagement on your Facebook page, Facebook puts your posts out into the news feed more often, so more of your fans and friends will see your posts. If your posts are not getting out into the news feed often, you are getting little to no engagement. That's the truth. But here's where I can make it extremely simple for you. When it comes to Facebook engagement, there are just four things Facebook is monitoring. You ready for this? Facebook is looking to see if your fans either:

1. Like your post.
2. Comment on your post
3. Share your post, or
4. Click a link in your post (if you include one, of course).

THAT IS IT. If Facebook users are not doing one of these four actions, Facebook thinks your audience is not at all interested in your content. If Facebook thinks your fans are not interested in your posts, they won't push your posts out into the news feed and your reach declines. Now do you see how reach and engagement go hand in hand?

#2: Guarantee Your Fans Will See Your Promotional Posts

Here's one more thing that most people teaching Facebook strategies fail to explain. When you increase your engagement by creating posts that get more engagement, you increase your chances of success when you promote and sell on Facebook. How does this work? The more often you create posts that elicit action (more likes, comments, shares and/or clicks) you are strengthening your reach and showing up more often in the news feed. That means that when you decide to promote or sell, those posts will ALSO get more reach and show up in the news feed. It's normal that posts that are promotional or selling won't get much engagement; however, if you make an effort to build up your engagement and reach with your non-promotional posts, when you promote, those posts get a free ride into the news feed. See how that works? Good stuff, right?

TWITTER

WHAT IT IS: Breaking news, quips and engagement: 140 characters to sound smart, funny and in-the-know. Retweet the ideas of people you find more intelligent, humorous and connected than you are. Launched in 2006 and by July 2014, 274 millions users were active on it and growing every day.

HOW IT WORKS BEST: See above.

STAR CHEFS: Again, kudos to Jamie Oliver (@jamieoliver) and Anthony Bourdain (@bourdain) for having the most followers of any celebrity chefs. Jamie has 4 million globally and Anthony has 1.9 million. Jamie uses Twitter to get even more personal with fans, sharing anecdotes about his family and travels around the globe. And Bourdain does what Bourdain does best...speaks frankly about what's on his mind whether it's revealing that "Ty Pennington's voice cuts into my brain like a Satanic dentist's drill" or "has no one noticed the racist anti-Muslim ads on the back of city buses? Pretty shameful shit, Mr. Mayor."

*Now is a good time to remind you that not everyone can get away with being so caustic. (See Adam Richman losing his television show for his less than gentlemanly response to a woman who admitted her dislike of the former *Man Vs. Food* star.) Being provocative can gain you fans. Being stupid and rude can lose those fans (and lucrative business deals) even faster.

Honorable Mention: Make sure you follow cookbook authors Michael Ruhlman, Dorie Greenspan and Mark Bittman.

Ruhlman (@ruhlman) entertains by ranting or raving about restaurants he's dining at as well as sending thought-provoking commentary about social issues that matter to him. (I adored his recent response to a woman asking if turkey bacon is a good substitute for bacon; "Google 'mechanically separated meat' then read turkey bacon ingredient. #wearesofuckedup.")

An unlikely Internet darling, baker and cook, Dorie Greenspan (@doriegreenspan) gained her fame and followers when a group of bloggers began baking every recipe from her cookbook *together* every week. She would join them via Twitter (and Skype and occasionally in person) to answer questions, provide encouragement and generally offer appreciation for their support of her work.

Bittman (@bittman) keeps you current with food issues and great recipes. All of these guys tweet back or retweet when you tweet them. Engaging with them will help you build your own following.

HOW IT CAN SELL YOUR COOKBOOK: It's amazing how so few words can be used to practically develop a complete media kit for your book. Take Mario Batali's (@mariobatali) use of Twitter to sell his latest cookbook *America Farm to Table* (Grand Central Publishing, 2014). He gave the book its own hashtag, #americafarmtotable, and is constantly tweeting reviews (@ibooks called it one of their new cookbooks we love), mentions from famous pals (Michael Symon and Robin Roberts), contests and book tour stops (which then morph into photos with fans, shout-outs to bookseller hosts and appreciative nods to the media who interview him in each city.) And before publication, Batali would tweet reminders of the book's publication date as well as links to a video of more traditional media appearances, such as his cooking demo on *Late Night With Jimmy Fallon*.

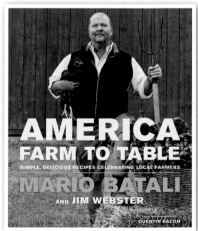

**Don't forget to mind your Ps and Qs with Twitter, too. Sure, Batali is a big star, but what makes him so successful on Twitter is that he's often giving shout-outs to others in social media and you know it's really him. Mario is a famous early riser. It's not uncommon for him to respond to your tweets before 6 a.m. as he heads to the studio to tape *The Chew*. Follow food people with big followings, retweet their ideas and add your voice into the mix. It will most definitely increase your chances of gaining new followers. You know the old maxim, it's better to give than receive? It's a little different when it comes to social media. You have to give to receive!

INSTAGRAM

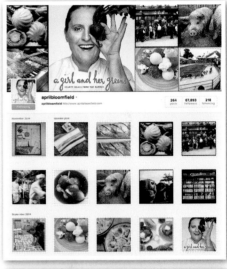

WHAT IT IS: An online mobile app that allows users to shares photos and 15-second videos on other social networking platforms like parent company Facebook, which acquired Instagram in 2012.

HOW IT WORKS BEST: Sharing visual proof of how well you eat and how great your life is. Instagram is the FOMO (fear of missing out) playground. For more information about the FOMO phenomenon, follow @caterina, founder of Flickr and most recently Findery, a brilliant Internet pioneer and one of my high school classmates and oldest friends—yep, I am name-dropping.

STAR CHEFS: April Bloomfield (@aprilbloomfield) and Tom Colicchio (@tcolic)

These two acclaimed chefs have been lauded for their Instagram pages by more than one social media outlet. Bloomfield, the reigning James Beard winner for "Best Chef in New York," shows her 65,800 followers really well-taken photos of her food, food she's eating elsewhere, cooking with other famous chefs, shooting scenes for PBS show *The Mind of a Chef*, making appearances at various award shows and lots and lots of pigs, fitting since her cookbook is titled *A Girl and Her Pig* (Ecco, 2012). I want to cook from her book after every post on her Instagram feed. Colicchio mostly shares gorgeous shots of food with his 40,301 followers, as well as promos for *Top Chef*, and every once in a while, you will see a childhood photo or him posing with a goat on the street.

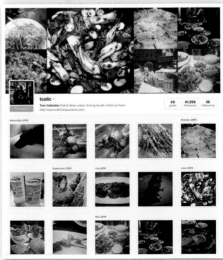

Honorable Mention: Be sure and check out the Instagram account of *Joy the Baker* (@joythebaker) as well. The self-taught LA blogger has 146,246 followers and photos that *Buzzfeed* said "will make your mouth water and have you running to your oven to try her recipes for yourself."

HOW IT CAN SELL YOUR COOKBOOK: As much as it pains me, I've got to give props to Real Housewife Bethenny Frankel for using Instagram to market each and every one of her products, whether it's a book or a bottle of Skinnygirl alcohol. She may get in trouble for some of her over-the-top behavior in real life, but she manages to toe the line well when it comes to promoting her products. At the moment, every post she sends on Instagram has a small icon of the current book she's promoting—a children's book called *Cookie Meets Peanut*. But she also makes sure to occasionally mention the name of her recent book, *Skinnygirl Cocktails* (Touchstone, 2014), as well as her products in ways that are appealing (i.e., one post has two martini glasses filled with a drink, with one of her bottles in the background... "anyone throwing a Halloween party this year? I love mixing @skinnygirl Bare Naked vodka with sparkling cider for a boozy fall treat.") Plus, Frankel remembers the 80–20 percent rule and makes sure that every photo isn't an excuse for product placement. She'll post a photo of what she's having for dinner, then ask her 333,899 followers to share what they're digging into that night. And believe me, they share.

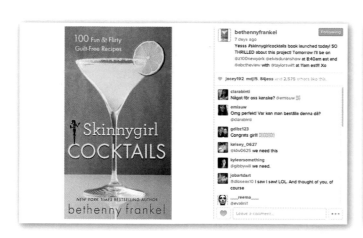

No surprise. It's all about the visuals on Instagram. If your photos are lame, you're lame, too. Even a perfectionist like Martha Stewart (@marthastewart) got hit with negative reviews for her laughably bad photos in November 2013! Help yourself take better photos by following the advice from Brooklyn-based food and wedding photographer and Instagram expert Daniel Krieger (@danielkrieger), who has worked for Eater.com, *The New York Times* and *Time Out New York*.

Spotlight:
Daniel Krieger's Tips for Taking Good Instagram Photos

1. Look for good light. "Professional photographers use elaborate and expensive lighting setups to create beautiful images, but that's not really an option for most people using their phones. The best thing to use is natural light. Window light is the first choice, but you can move yourself around to find what's right—sometimes it takes a few minutes and a few tries to really get it perfect. There's something magical about the way the iPhone picks up direct light on food, creating beautiful colors and shadows."

2. Put some distance between you and your subject. "I find a lot of the worst food photos happen because people are way too close to their food. Cameras in phones don't do macro well, so back the fuck up! For most of my food or cocktail photos, I like to be a few feet away from my subject. Experiment with a range of two to four feet away and see how it looks. Obviously, if you're photographing a small cupcake you'll want to be closer—or just get a bigger cupcake."

3. Watch your peripherals. "Try keeping the table clean except for a few essential details: the dish, maybe a napkin, silverware and a drink."

4. Try a bird's-eye-view shot. "This is my go-to style of shooting. With my professional camera I have more flexibility with lenses to create different looks, but the camera in an iPhone looks great when shooting from above."

5. Experiment, and take a bunch of shots. "Try moving yourself around what you're shooting—the food is going to stay still, but you can move yourself. Find the right light by shooting different angles and locations. Fire off a few frames; don't just take one photo. Try the edge of a table—I like incorporating angles and patterns in my images when possible. And finally, edit the image: Snapseed is a powerful and free editing tool, and I edit just about every photograph I post to Instagram.

PINTEREST

WHAT IT IS: The newest success story in social media, the free web and mobile app is a visual scrapbook of inspiration. It launched in 2010 and now has over 70 million users—the majority of them are female.

HOW IT WORKS BEST: This is a great visual way to highlight your versatility—whether it's the food you like to cook, the random objects you collect or the beautiful sights you see.

STAR CHEFS: Martha Stewart and Andrew Zimmern (just type their names into the search to see all of their boards).

Of course, the queen of domestic perfection aces Pinterest. (Clearly, she learned from the 2013 digs at her online photography skills—that and an entire staff of brilliant editorial people working on her boards.) Her 232,965 followers can check out boards featuring her beloved pets, gorgeous gardens, jadeite collection and behind-the-scenes photos at the office. *Bizarre Foods*' Zimmern meanwhile entertains his 51,211 followers with cookbook and restaurant recommendations, photos of his amazing travels and specific recipe collections from his ideas for brunch to a Super Bowl party. My favorite board of his is "21 Meals To Try Before You Die."

HOW IT CAN SELL YOUR COOKBOOK: All of us in the food world have just begun to scratch the surface of how to use Pinterest but it's critical to get pinning (it's also fast becoming the number-one place to search recipes online). PEW Research believes that it will catch up to Twitter in popularity very soon. The goal is to have your photos repinned on as many group boards as possible. (See explanation below.) Right now, Tiffany McCauley, the creator of The Gracious Pantry, a blog that details her transformation to a diet of nonprocessed foods, could be the most skilled Pinner using the site right now. Her "Clean Eating" photos are on 243 different boards and she's been pinned 16,897 times (compared to Martha Stewart's 31 boards and 2,699 pins!). It helps that her recipe ideas can be placed in so many categories, from types of cuisine, to specific holidays, to grocery lists at various stores. Frankly, it's nearly impossible to browse the food at Pinterest and not run into her.

*The explanation is excerpted from social media consultant Tehmina Zaman's online article, "How to Use Pinterest's Group Boards to Get More Exposure for Your Business."

Group boards are not only a great way to organize ideas and bring people together, but they can also have real tangible benefits for your brand and business.

#1. Dramatically boost your followers. If users select to "follow all" of any contributor's boards, then they will be added as followers to a group board you are part of. The increased exposure and visibility you get through boards will increase your follower growth at a faster rate.

#2. Exponentially increase the number of repins. The more followers you have the more likely they (and their followers) are to see your content, repin your pins and click through to your website. This means more traffic to your site and potentially more subscribers, customers and clients.

#3. Put your pinning virtually on autopilot. Implement this strategy correctly and you could get other people creating content for you. Certainly at the start, Pinterest can be time-consuming. But managed well, you could soon have a team of people perpetuating your content for you across their networks.

#4. Increase engagements and create brand ambassadors. Your customers may already be liking, commenting and sharing your content with their followers on Pinterest. But inviting them to pin your brand's group board will get them more engaged and involved in your online conversation.

Still confused about the difference between Instagram and Pinterest? Read this post from Danielle Cormier, a social media community manager at Constant Contact:

With Pinterest, a user's intent is primarily focused on the discovery and curation of other users' content. Similar to a search engine, users can use Pinterest to search for specific content or products. They can then create visually appealing boards by pinning and grouping the content they discover.

On Pinterest, every pin is a link to the source of the image, usually an external site. Therefore, one of the common goals for businesses is generating website traffic and using Pinterest for Search Engine Optimization purposes. Pinterest is also a proven sales generator for retail businesses.

On Instagram, users are looking for a much more personal experience with the brands they follow and engage with. The content you share on Instagram should give your audience an authentic view into your business.

YOUTUBE

WHAT IT IS: A video-sharing website that's been around since 2005. It became a subsidiary of Google in 2006.

HOW IT WORKS BEST: Show off your chops in the kitchen via a cooking demo or your overall ability to charm, entertain and perform in front of a camera.

STAR CHEFS: Lately Youtube has launched the careers of more than a few culinary stars. It's important to note that more than on any other platform, collaboration is a critical component to success—my favorites have appeared with many of their YouTuber colleagues, sharing audiences and generally having a grand old time. Even Jamie Oliver's FoodTube (youtube.com/user/jamieoliver) is a place for Jamie to be on TV with friends and fellow YouTubers. Here are some of my favorites:

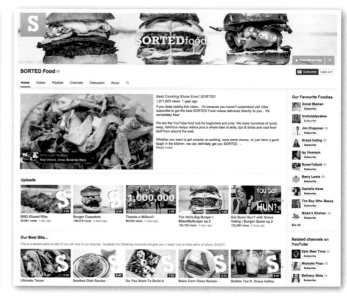

Hannah Hart (www.youtube.com/user/mydrunkkitchen)**:** In March 2011, Hart shot a video of herself drinking wine and trying to make a grilled cheese sandwich. The catch? She didn't have any cheese. She posted the video on YouTube, called her channel "My Drunk Kitchen" and the episode "Butter Your Shit" got 800,000 hits in three months! Now she has 1.4 million subscribers and celebrity guests like Mary Louise Parker and *The Fault in Our Stars* author John Green, who also wrote the foreword to her new parody cookbook, *My Drunk Kitchen: A Guide to Eating, Drinking and Going With Your Gut* (Dey Street Books, August 2014).

Sorted (www.youtube.com/sortedfood)**:** Jamie Spafford, Ben Ebbrell, Barry Taylor and Mike Huttlestone are the pioneers of YouTube Food sensation Sorted Food. It's a very simple formula. Ebbrell, the sole member with any cooking chops, recommends simple and cheap recipes for the others to try and people go crazy for it. The channel has over 850,000 subscribers and has led to four cookbooks and they are now regular guests on *Today* on NBC.

Tastemade is a platform worth exploring, too. A multichannel network, app and complete production studio make this LA start-up a veritable incubator of cooking talent.

HOW IT CAN SELL YOUR COOKBOOK: Ask any media executive what they're spending money and energy on right now and they'll tell you it's video. And you should too, especially when it comes to promoting your cookbook. Cookbooks have trailers now, just like feature films. You can see New Orleans's chef John Besh offering a straightforward walk through his culinary history to show you what his book *Cooking from the Heart* (Andrews McMeel Publishing, 2013) will include. There's also Allison and Matt Robicelli starring in a quirky low-tech video where they frolic in a park with animated cupcakes to introduce you to *Robicelli's: A Love Story, with Cupcakes*. And don't miss the Mast Brothers trailer for their first cookbook, *Mast Brothers Chocolate: A Family Cookbook* with a foreword by Thomas Keller (Little Brown & Company, October 2013.)

But the real success story here is Michelle Davis and Matt Holloway, the creators of the vegan blog Thug Kitchen. Granted, they've taken some real flack for appropriating the word 'thug' since they are a white couple from Orange County, California, but I suspect their hilarious video trailer, which parodies those annoyingly earnest drug commercials, for their book *Thug Kitchen* (Rodale, 2014) helped them get to the top spot on *The New York Times* bestseller list as well as number-one vegan cookbook—that and the zillions in their online community. The trailer was funny, subversive and expressed the philosophy and attitude behind their ideas.

Mast Brothers

So, what have we learned from our brief travels through the most traveled social media sites? These platforms are undeniably the most effective way to showcase your talents, while also proving that your unique awesomeness doesn't prevent you from relating to—and being liked by—all the other people in the world using social media as well.

Chapter 9

Old School: Book Tours, Nationals and the Brave New Frontier of Traditional Media

∽

Cue Bruce Springsteen singing, "Glory Days." It used to be so easy to propel a cookbook to a bestseller: Secure a few great advance magazine placements, think features in *Bon Appetit, InStyle* and maybe *Martha Stewart* and *Real Simple*, too, then book a couple of great newspapers features—*USA Today, The New York Times*. Then maybe a nice story on the wire, book a national television placement or two—*Today* was the reigning king and only two hours long, or you could get lucky with Regis or Letterman, and then book 5 to 10 key market cities on a book tour. And while the author is on the road, supplement with radio phone interviews and other newspapers around the country. And watch it work. Your book would start climbing up regional bestseller lists, and then if you're lucky, crack the *Publishers Weekly* list and maybe, just maybe, you'd hit *The New York Times* bestseller list. And you were set. Don't get me wrong, it wasn't easy, there were lots (lots!) of phone calls to make and faxes to send—remember no email in the early 1990s—but if you were diligent and had a good book, a game plan and a mediagenic author, you could make some magic happen.

Now you can almost never generate enough publicity—and rarely will publicity alone create a bestseller. You have to do everything possible to promote your cookbook everywhere possible and support it with an integrated marketing campaign that can include everything from Facebook ads to Amazon promotions to media partnerships with new media players like *Buzzfeed* or *Vice*. As we've discussed, the media landscape has shifted in one million big and small ways. Competition is much fiercer for the coveted national television spots and even when you land one, sales are not guaranteed. And across the board the number of books sold has decreased by an order of magnitude.

But don't give up yet. The Fat Lady hasn't started singing. Publicity is still important and a strategic campaign with targeted results will sell books. This chapter will teach you how to create and execute a PR (with some limited marketing ideas thrown in for good measure) campaign—whether you hire a professional to execute (and you know I suggest that you do) or do it yourself, you need to understand how the media works and how you can work best with them.

The Book Tour

Let's start with the book tour, because it is still by far my favorite and the most effective publicity tool you have. The only downside to a book tour is that it's expensive. You will need to budget for travel (and extra baggage fees because you are a cook, and a cook needs to bring her tools), lodging and on-the-ground support, which includes everything from ground transportation to grocery shopping, food styling, hair and makeup as well as a solid budget to entertain the important journalists in each market.

Planning for your book tour should begin six months in advance. You need to select your cities and pick your dates. Make sure you find out which other books are being published around the same time so you can avoid bumping into the competition on the road. One quick perusal of my Instagram feed the third week of October 2014, showed a veritable all-star team of cookbook authors on tour—a few in the same cities on the same day! We're talking big, bestselling, media-hogging stars, like Mario Batali, Ina Garten, Tyler Florence, Marcus Sameulsson, Dominique Ansel, Dorie Greenspan, Sean Brock, Yotam Ottolenghi and Italy's number-one chef, Massimo Bottura.

They were making national television appearances, local television appearances, radio interviews, newspaper interviews, doing book signings and talks—many in big venues—all while tweeting, Instagramming, live chatting and flogging their book in every online outlet possible. Cookbook tours are becoming more like concert tours than ever before. Mario Batali, Tyler Florence and Dominique Ansel kicked off their tours at the *Delicious Food Show* (www.deliciousfood.com) in Toronto with stage demonstrations, book signings and lots of free advertising from the show's promoter. Thousands of tickets were sold, and not only did the promoters guarantee a minimum number of books sold, they often pay appearance fees and all of the travel expenses for the author to attend.

New and lesser known authors rarely get this royal treatment, however they can and should model their tours in the very same fashion.

Look at it this way—the big stars are only going to markets where the fish are—so a good way to choose your markets is to see where the competition is going and go there too—just on a different day—preferably a sunny day where you are the only one in town of any fame whatsoever—obviously for New York and Los Angeles that will be nearly impossible, but totally doable in smaller markets.

The best cities for cookbooks haven't changed that much over the years and I have created a little algorithm to choose the best cities for an individual title. I start with cities that have strong local media—at least one local television morning show that will book guests for in-studio appearances, a widely read local newspaper that can promote an event in advance, as well as offer coverage when the author is in the city. Types of this coverage include: cookbook reviews, feature stories with interviews, recipe excerpts, questions-and-answers, or at the very least, small mentions announcing the book's publication, including a photo of the jacket. These stories run in online editions as well, and are very helpful in selling books and driving traffic to local in-market events. The city should also have an active food blogging community, be considered a foodie city, and if you're lucky, have a couple of local radio shows, preferably an NPR station that will book in-studio interviews.

The best cookbook tour cities include New York, Los Angeles (where it is actually very hard to book interviews unless you are a celebrity), Chicago, San Francisco, Atlanta, Houston and Seattle. Depending on the subject of the cookbook, these cities can be good, too: Nashville, Miami, Dallas, Boston, Minneapolis and Denver.

Once you've created a short list, cross-reference that with your personal network as well as the subject of the book. If the book is about Southern cooking, obviously you want to visit Southern cities. If there is a special health focus, do some research into cities that have large communities of Paleo or Macrobiotic or specialty diet interest. Think like a marketer. You are looking for a heavy concentration of your target demographic. Remember you're trying to fish where the fish are.

And finding the fish has never been easier. The best thing about the social media revolution is the sheer amount of data now available about your personal network. Through Google and Facebook analytics, you know who your people are and where they are coming from. Bring the show to them. Use them as market research. For example, if you are planning a trip to Denver in the fall, put out a call on Facebook in the spring to survey the best venues. Ask you network where they want to see you and what they want you to do. Do they want you to teach? Do a lecture? Eat your food at a restaurant? If so, which restaurant? The people in your network are your greatest resource and as you have spent the last year giving to them and nurturing their growth, it is time to activate the return on investment now and, of course, at publication date.

Bestselling cookbook author Dorie Greenspan is one of the best in the business at nurturing her network. She took the opportunity to energize her fan base right before she hit the road for her extensive book tour to promote *Baking Chez Moi* (Houghton Mifflin Harcourt, October 2014). On October 8, 2014, in a blog post on www.doriegreenspan.com, she wrote:

> So here's where we're at: *Baking Chez Moi* will be published in 19 days (not that I have a calendar that I'm crossing off days on or anything). And when that happens, I'll tuck a book under my arm and start traveling the country.
>
> I'm **posting my tour dates and venues HERE** (http://doriegreenspan .com/baking-chez-moi-tour-schedule.html), so it will always be easily available. (I'll update it as I get more information on the places I'll be.)
>
> I love going on a **book tour** because I love meeting YOU! Please, if we're going to be near one another, come say hello—it'll be great to have a chance to chat. As you'll see on the tour page, I'll be in New York City, San Francisco, Vancouver, Seattle, Los Angeles, Milwaukee, Chicago, all over Connecticut, Boston, Washington, DC, Bethesda, MD and Princeton, NJ.
>
> See you soon—xoDorie

> PS: Remember that when you preorder your book, you can send a copy of your receipt to **hmhcooks@gmail.com** and my publisher, Houghton Mifflin Harcourt, will send you a Baking Chez Moi tea towel. You can preorder books from anywhere—and electronic books count!
>
> PPS: If you'd like to join the fabulous online baking group, Tuesdays with Dorie, they're setting up a bake-along for *Baking Chez Moi*. It will start the first week of November. More info here (http://tuesdayswithdorie.wordpress.com/2014/10/01/ exciting-news/#comments).
>
> OK, last word: Doesn't "Baking Chez Moi: The Tour" sound so rock'n'roll? Love it!

In this post, Dorie does everything right (ask anyone who knows her and they will tell you that in general, Dorie does everything right). She communicates her tour to the fans, asks them to come see her, promotes her online baking club (which has been one of her key drivers to the bestseller list) and even offers her community a gift if they preorder the book. Here's an inside secret: Big preorders for your book will debut you on a bestseller list. Essentially all of those preorders get recorded for the first day on sale, inflating your first week's sale to way more than what it would be if those numbers weren't counted. Additionally, *Publishers Weekly* takes QVC numbers into their list so that is yet one more reason publishers like to book QVC.

If you take the time to review her tour, you will see that she's booked a variety of events, ticketed and non-ticketed, talks, classes and demonstrations. She's usually doing more than one event in each market and as of one week before her tour, many were sold out.

Another factor to consider when planning your tour is what potential partners you can activate to help. "Help" can take many forms and include dollars, promotion, a large book order, and even advertising campaigns. It all depends on the nature of the partnership and the incentive for both sides.

West Elm is a major advertiser for the website Apartment Therapy. When Apartment Therapy's The Kitchn published their first cookbook, *The Kitchn Cookbook* (Clarkson Potter, October 2014) by Sara Kate Gillingham and Faith Durand, West Elm created a partnership that included a $2,000 kitchen makeover sweepstakes, book tour and subscriber promotion—plus a large book order. West Elm kicked off the tour with a media-filled book party at the New York City flagship store and toured the authors (separately) to Chicago, Dallas, Houston, Columbus, OH (Faith's hometown), Los Angeles and Philadelphia. The Kitchn actively promoted each event and added West Elm in the "Where to Buy" section of the website. This partnership was a win-win. West Elm was looking to increase their kitchen business (they're not just sheets and throws) and The Kitchn got a national promotional partner. In this case, West Elm picked the cities for the book tour and used all of its customer analytics, cross-referenced with The Kitchn's, to find the best markets.

National gourmet retailer Williams-Sonoma aggressively courts publishers to host events for their key authors and the fall season of 2014 brought them quite a coup. They were the exclusive sponsor of mega-bestselling cookbook author Ina Garten. Here's the promo from their website:

Williams-Sonoma Proudly Presents
Ina Garten's Make it Ahead Tour
Boston, Chicago, Cupertino, Denver and Beverly Hills

> Beloved culinary icon INA GARTEN is coming to a city near you! The author of eight bestselling cookbooks and host of the Food Network's "Barefoot Contessa Back to Basics" show—winner of both Emmy and James Beard awards—is celebrating the release of her eagerly anticipated ninth book, *Make It Ahead: A Barefoot Contessa Cookbook*.

Joined by a local moderator, Ina will share behind-the-scene stories of filming her award-winning television show, writing her bestselling cookbooks, and enjoying food with family and friends at her home in the Hamptons. An audience Q & A will immediately follow each interview.

Purchase Tickets and Preorder an Autographed Cookbook for Pickup at Event!

WILLIAMS-SONOMA is proud to be the **exclusive** bookseller of *Make It Ahead: A Barefoot Contessa Cookbook* for these exciting events. We are now offering ticket holders autographed copies of Ina's new book for purchase online to be picked up at the event.

To purchase tickets and preorder an autographed book, select a city from the list below.

Please note: event tickets and signed books are sold separately. You must have an event ticket to pick up your preordered book.

Williams-Sonoma also hosts a number of less marquee events and there are opportunities for emerging authors to teach classes and do demonstrations. The independent booksellers that continue to thrive have made events critical to their success. Trust The Vero Beach Books Center in Vero Beach, Florida, Books & Books in Miami and Coral Gables, Book Soup in Los Angeles, Vroman's in Pasadena, Parnassus Books in Nashville and Book Passage in Corte Madera, California, to do a great job hosting your event.

Barnes & Noble has created a compelling format for questions and answers with high-profile authors in a number of cities across the country. It's important to mix up your choices—and don't play favorites (you're not Ina Garten yet!). Central Market in Dallas hosts visiting authors for cooking classes, Anthropologie can be a good option for the right book, many chefs will host other chefs for a Cook the Book series, including Suzanne Goin in Los Angeles, Marc Vetri in Philadelphia and Jonathan Waxman in New York City. Private clubs do a great job, too. The Junior Leagues across the south and in Texas will host visiting authors. The 92nd Street Y in NYC and The Commonwealth Club in San Francisco have great series with chefs. Soho House in New York, Los Angeles, Miami and Chicago will host restaurant and speaking events and in some clubs, hands-on classes, too. The Viceroy Hotels bring big names to their Anguilla property, and of course don't forget the OG cooking schools, Sur La Table (in many markets), Let's Get Cookin' in Westlake Village, California, The Southern Season in Charleston as well as the Viking Cooking Studios that have popped up across the country.

These events must be planned at least four months in advance and many much earlier to make the printing dates for their calendars. You want to choose hosts with proven track records for success and ask that they demonstrate in advance how they are going to do a good job getting the people through the door.

Checklist for a Great Event

To execute a great public event, you need to do a lot of the work yourself. Don't expect your publisher or your host to move heaven and earth to get a crowd for your appearance. They are depending on you to be the draw. Here are some questions to ask your host:

▷ How big is their mailing list?

▷ How active are they on social media?

▷ How connected are they to local media?

▷ Will they be doing any advertising in support of and in advance of your event?

▷ What will the in-store merchandising look like and for how long in advance of your appearance, and after your appearance, will it be up?

▷ How can you plug your social network and channels into their marketing mix?

▷ Will they be serving food from the book at the event? If so, who is going to cook it? And dear God, what is it going to look and taste like? This lesson was learned by me the hard way—on more than one occasion. You may want to either supervise the cooking or request they serve their "house favorites" versus recipes from your book. Even though you've tested the recipes innumerable times and they are foolproof, don't trust they will be executed exactly as the recipe specifies.

⏩ Will tickets be sold or given away? How will the ticket sales be promoted, how much will they cost and what will that get the guest? Will the book be included as part of the sale?

⏩ What assets do they need and how far in advance?

The final step is setting your budget and making the hard decisions. How many markets can you afford, and how many books will you need to sell to make it worth the investment?

Creating Your Own Media Kit

It's very important to have a collection of digital assets at the ready for your book. You will need:

⏩ Jpeg of book jacket, high-resolution and low-resolution

⏩ Short-and long-form biographies

⏩ Author photograph

⏩ Small collection of recipes and photos

⏩ Media reel—including live television appearances

⏩ General press release about your book

Additionally you should work out your key message points—the three or four main ideas that make your book unique and newsworthy, and a couple of pitch ideas for your publicist at the ready.

Media Training

Giving good TV demo is an absolutely essential skill you need. You need to shine, and to shine you need practice. Getting comfortable in front of the camera, like any other skill, is learned. Throughout the course of developing your recipes for the book, you should force yourself to videotape your efforts at least one day a week. Set up your phone or a little camera on a tripod—or have a friend come over and film you in return for a nice meal. Work toward a 4-minute demo—so be smart about which recipes you choose. You want a simple recipe that showcases your cooking style and unique selling proposition, but also one that doesn't require more than two swaps to get to the finished product. You want to cook in real time as much as possible. And if you start to get segments you like, take some time to learn how to do some minimal editing and cut a few pieces together to become content for your social media channels. Remember: Good content never goes to waste.

One month before your book publishes, schedule some professional media training. A coach will work with you and your recipe to perfect your key message points, the flow of your demo and the timing of the segment.

America's Media Markets

It's important to understand markets and their rankings, as well as metrics for measuring their reach. According to Wikipedia, "a media market, broadcast market, media region, designated market area (DMA), television market area, or simply a market, is a region where the population can receive the same (or similar) television and radio station offerings, and may also include other types of media including newspapers and Internet content.

They are widely used in audience measurements, which are compiled in the United States by Nielsen Media Research. Nielsen measures both television and radio audiences since its acquisition of Arbitron. Markets are identified by the largest city, which is usually located in the center of the market region. However, geography and the fact that some metropolitan areas have large cities separated by some distance can make markets have unusual shapes and result in two, three or more names being used to identify a single region (such as Wichita-Hutchison, Kansas; Chico-Redding, California; Albany-Schenectady-Troy, New York; and Harrisburg-Lebanon-Lancaster-York, Pennsylvania."

These rankings are important to know because on a book tour you are trying to generate as many media impressions as possible.

Media impressions are tricky bits of business, because PR agencies are always playing around with the numbers to try to generate the most impressions possible. Christopher S. Penn, vice president of marketing technoloy for Shift Communications (www.shiftcomm.com), does a great job describing it in a blog post in April, 2014:

> "One of the most common metrics talked about in traditional public relations as well as advertising is the media impression. However, it's not always clear what an impression is or why it matters, not to mention, some folks believe impressions don't matter at all. Let's dig into this metric and understand what it truly measures.
>
> Impressions, broadly defined, are any interaction with a piece of content and an audience member. For example, when you read the front page of *The New York Times*, every article on that page counts your viewing as one impression. When you drive past a billboard on a highway, that counts as an impression. When you read Facebook, every ad that scrolls by in your news feed is an impression. An impression is the broadest possible metric for any piece of earned, owned, or paid media's performance.
>
> With such a broad definition, do impressions count for anything? In the biggest possible picture, they do matter a little—after all, if you have a choice between having your media be seen by one person or one million people, the logical choice (all other factors being equal) is to choose the larger audience.

Think of impressions as a directional metric. If you're out there working to get publicity about a story, product, idea or service, and your impressions count is zero, then the rest of your PR and marketing metrics aren't going to look great either. Impressions bridge the gap between the world and the total addressable audience that you have and the rest of your PR and marketing funnel.

The reason why impressions are given a bad rap is that many advertising and PR measurement efforts stop at impressions. Impressions are only the very top of the funnel—much more has to happen after an impression of an ad is served or a story is displayed. Just because someone has driven by a billboard doesn't mean they will remember it. If you're not hungry, chances are you aren't going to pay attention to a fast food restaurant sign.

So what should you logically measure after the impression? **Engagement.** Did someone pay attention? In digital PR and advertising, this is more easily measured than offline. Metrics can range from simple behaviors like 'bounce rate' and 'time on page' to more complex metrics like 'branded organic search over time' and 'social media engagement.'

After engagement, we must measure **conversion**. Who did what we wanted them to do? From walking into a store and picking up an item to clicking through to the story or filling out a form. What tangible, measurable, impactful thing did the audience do next that advances the business?

It's important to emphasize that impressions do matter; they're the 'once upon a time' of your earned media story. **Impressions help us set the context for everything that comes after.** Just as a child wouldn't be satisfied with a bedtime story that ended after 'once upon a time,' nor should we be satisfied with impressions being the only metric reported. However, a bedtime story that didn't start with 'once upon a time' would equally feel incomplete. Our measurement of earned, owned and paid media feels just as incomplete without that big picture audience understanding."

Booksellers have metrics too—they are book sales! Amazon and BN.com do live rankings and booksellers report sales to Bookscan, which publishers subscribe to so they can find out what is working in the marketplace on any given day. You want your media placements to yield spikes in your sales numbers, obviously.

National Media That Matters

Even in the current media landscape, nothing gives you more eyeballs then securing a national television booking. The best shows for cookbooks include *Dr. Oz*, *Good Morning America*, *Today* (preferably in the first three hours), *CBS This Morning*, *Live! With Kelly & Michael*, *The View*, *Ellen*, *The Chew*, *Rachael Ray* and *The Talk*. If you have a newsworthy book or are famous talent, then the late-night shows are an option, too. *The Tonight Show With Jimmy Fallon* and *Jimmy Kimmel Live!*

All shows are booked by producers. Some shows have "talent departments" that handle all guest bookings. while the morning shows have "book producers" who handle all of the bookings. Your publicist, or you, should send packages to the right person with a personalized letter and link to another appearance. It is very rare that a show will book a new author without some kind of tape—the media training tape will work. The shows are extremely competitive and want exclusive or first options on the talent. For example, if you book the third hour of *Today*, then *Live! with Kelly & Michael* won't put you on. It's very tricky terrain and one where are you served to have a professional guiding your pitches. It is only in the rarest case will a new author get booked without a publicist—although miracles do happen. See the Matt Moore story on the next page.

Words of Wisdom:
Be Your Own Best Publicist

A study in luck and hard work from Matt Moore

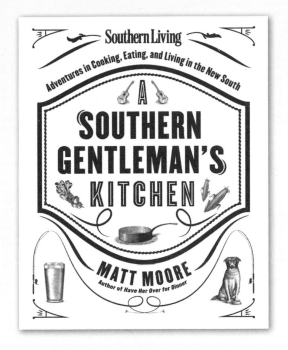

Matt Moore is a Nashville musician, author and entrepreneur. Always a good cook, he often entertained friends, family and countless dates. He began getting requests for recipes—lots and lots of requests—from his single friends looking to impress women. Ever the entrepreneur, this working musician realized he should put all of his hard-earned knowledge into a book and try to sell it. At the very least, he could stop the 200 or so individual emails he sent each year offering free advice and recipes. He self-published his first book *Have Her Over For Dinner* in 2010 (just before the self-publishing revolution) which *The New York Times* named one of the best books of the year. He shot 90 percent of the photos himself, hired a local graphic designer he found on Craigslist, who was looking for some work for her portfolio and able to work on a small budget. He got a family friend/English professor to help him with the final edit and made sure the product was the highest quality possible—no typos, quality photos, engaging design. He went to print and got to work promoting his book.

What differentiates Matt from many self-published authors is not only his work ethic, and enough Southern charm to get just about anyone to do anything for him, but his strategic vision for his launch. We have the privilege on working on Matt's second book, *Southern Living: A Southern Gentleman's Kitchen*: *Adventures in Cooking, Eating, and Living in The New South* (Oxmoor House, April 2015), and we're going to have to really bring our A game to do a better job than he did for himself. Matt was generous enough to share his gameplan with us here:

▷ "Credibility is critical to any successful publicity campaign. I needed to establish who I was, what need my book solved, and why I was the perfect guy to do it. I used the book as my collateral to create credibility. My book was an all-in-one marketing and credibility play.

▷ You can't have a successful business venture selling to family and friends. No matter how big your family or network is, it's simply going to fail if you don't have a wider reach. Ninety-five percent of self-published authors don't ever sell more than 5,000 copies.

(continued)

» I never had the budget to hire a publicist so I had to figure it out myself. My plan was to start small and build from there. I began with the bloggers. I started looking at all the blogs that spoke to my niche—single guys, divorced guys, guys from 18 to 50. I compiled a list and practiced my pitch on the smaller ones first. I had great content to pitch and I found many of them very receptive to my offer. Once I got a few posts, I would use those as proof of good content for larger blogs. All I asked in return was a byline and/or link to my book's Amazon page. I found that most bloggers are pretty personable now, and if you have an earnest pitch and you've got good content to back it up you will get placements. And I did. And then I moved into the next phase.

» Because of my experience in the music business, I knew you could break things locally in your home market. I started with the local Nashville papers, and worked my way up to the city and regional magazines, all the way up to *At Home Tennessee*. Keep in mind the magazines have a long lead time, so once I got confirmed in them, I used those placements as the news hook to pitch TV in the Nashville market. Little by little, I built my reel and press clippings that I posted on my new blog.

» Once I had exhausted Nashville, I worked out in concentric circles. I hit Atlanta, Memphis and Knoxville. Granted, not all of the markets were home runs, but I managed to get myself on TV, featured in local papers and blogs and started selling my book directly to the local bookstores.

» After the success in the South, I pitched WGN in Chicago—one of the smaller national television shows. Once I did that successfully, I set my eyes on the prize and began my inroads with the national media in New York and Los Angeles.

» I started emailing top folks in a very courteous way. Whenever possible, I would send handwritten notes in advance of the email to set the tone of the relationship. I had experience but wasn't known enough to get a return call. I had to be patient and work it. I sent a carefully curated package, and followed up, and in the process began to create relationships.

One of those relationships was with Julia Moskin of *The New York Times*. I sent her my book and clips and gently followed up throughout the fall. My persistence paid off when she included me in her list of Best Cookbooks of 2010.

And that was just the big break I needed. Now I had one more reason to follow up with the national producers. I had a book I was very proud of and one that had just been anointed by the paper of record. *The New York Times* piece changed everything for me. The producers began responding and I got booked for a segment on the *Today* show.

I credit my success to a great product, hard work and a little luck. Probably what most entrepreneurs would say. What most entrepreneurs wouldn't say though, and what I think is very important, is that no matter how much money you spend on something, if it's not good and doesn't solve a need that the market needs you should scrap it and come up with something better."

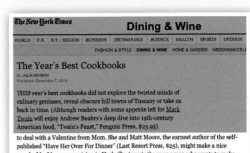

The New York Times

Dining & Wine

WORLD   U.S.   N.Y. / REGION   BUSINESS   TECHNOLOGY   SCIENCE   HEALTH   SPORTS   OPINION

FASHION & STYLE   **DINING & WINE**   HOME & GARDEN   WEDDINGS/CELI

The Year's Best Cookbooks

By JULIA MOSKIN
Published: December 7, 2010

THIS year's best cookbooks did not explore the twisted minds of culinary geniuses, reveal obscure hill towns of Tuscany or take us back in time. (Although readers with some appetite left for Mark Twain will enjoy Andrew Beahrs's deep dive into 19th-century American food, "Twain's Feast," Penguin Press, $25.95).

to deal with a Valentine from Mom. She and Matt Moore, the earnest author of the self-published "Have Her Over For Dinner" (Last Resort Press, $25), might make a nice couple. Mr. Moore, a musician in Nashville, targets the young man who wants to make dinner on a date — while managing to avoid the usual Playboy-tinged prose of cookbooks "for men."

Tony Cenicola/The New York Times

HOLIDAY
Gift Guide **2010**

A selection of gift ideas from The New York Times.

Florence Fabricant's Selected New Products »
Go to the Holiday Gift Guide »

"Heart of the Artichoke" is the follow-up to "A Platter of Figs" (both Artisan, $35). Despite his triply enviable lifestyle (Paris resident, part-time chef at Chez Panisse, frequent traveler to Morocco and Mexico), Mr. Tanis is also a highly practical adviser to American home cooks. His tricks for improving supermarket steak (rub it with garlic and salt) and making pasta for one person (cook it like risotto) will inscribe themselves on your brain. Mr. Tanis's gifts for composing menus and conveying kitchen wisdom are on every page, along with some perfect sentences like "Sheep, it turns out, adore bread." (This is followed by the unimprovable opening: "When I worked as a cook in a chateau in the Dordogne. ...")

The Review Mailing

Traditionally, book publishers send a good number of review copies to all of the book reviewers at newspapers across the country, which is how this mailing got its name. For cookbooks, it is the "big list" of media who you want to cover your book and can include newspaper food editors, online outlets, magazine editors, radio producers and bloggers. Your publicist will create a list with all of the best people on it, and include at the very least a book and the press release. Packages can also include a more expanded press kit which includes the author bio, targeted pitch letter and sample recipes.

Blogger Campaign

As we all know, bloggers are a very important group to rally around your book at publication. As we also all know, there are zillions of bloggers with readerships ranging from five to hundreds of thousands—so choosing the right collection of bloggers to pitch is the science and knowing what to offer them is a fine art. Aimée Bianca, the chief media relations officer at my company is absolutely brilliant at finding and pitching the right bloggers. She's generously given me permission to share her process (and our trade secrets!) here. This works equally well for traditional media, too.

Spotlight:
Aimée Bianca's Signature Process: BUILD A BETTER LIST–AKA NO MORE LAZY LISTS

Now that Matt Moore has shown you anyone can be a publicist—here's a primer from a professional, and one of the best in the business—my own chief media relations officer, Aimée Bianca.

It starts with fanaticism—constantly taking note of new outlets, new bloggers, new columns. I rip pages out of magazines, send emails to myself in the middle of the night, scroll through Twitter feeds, etc.

▶ It may seem crazy, but there's a method to all of the madness.

Why good targeted lists are so important

▶ Is your book pitch getting no response? Chances are you didn't send the book to the right person.

▶ There's nothing worse to a journalist than you not knowing what they cover. Journalists expect professionalism—and knowing what they write about is the cost of entry of our job.

▶ Aimée's lists are so good that even the UPS man remarked that we don't get return packages compared to other people who ship as much as we do.

▶ Each campaign requires a new fresh list to be successful. Journalists and bloggers are always moving around.

Rely on your brain, not media databases

▷ Media databases are tools to identify to find the contacts and research outlets, but the magic in list making comes from having a game plan first, an idea of what you are trying to extrapolate from the database.

▷ What are you trying to accomplish with your campaign? Do you want people to review your book, interview you, do a giveaway, excerpt recipes? And then find the person who does exactly that thing.

How you do it

▷ Identify the top media in traditional and digital.

▷ READ. Stay abreast of what people are covering and writing about. Pay attention to bylines.

▷ Recognize the writers—key not just to the task at hand but to building relationships.

Beyond the database

▷ Google competitors—i.e., everyone who has covered the Dorie Greenspan book if you are publishing a baking book.

▷ Press pages on websites—everybody shows! Anyone in the food world with a site who gets press and has it up for the world to see.

▷ See what PR companies are booking by stalking social media channels.

▷ What kind of coverage in the Twittersphere or Instagram world—who are getting congratulations and shout-outs, what articles or pieces are being retweeted?

▷ Head down the research rabbit hole—look through Twitter followers of your competitors and follow their followers. Read their feeds, click through the links, take note of names of people writing, and then contact them on your own behalf.

Satellite Media Tours

Satellite Media Tours come in two types: television (SMT) and radio (RMT) tours. They are an efficient way to reach 13 to 15 television markets—and can cost from $15,000 to $50,000, depending on the location and setup. Typically a cookbook author will go into a studio and in front of a kitchen set do a demo or point and chat to a selection of recipes from the book and be interviewed live (or live-to-tape) to local television morning shows. For example, when Morgan Murphy published *Bourbon & Bacon* (Oxmoor House, September 2014), Clyde May's Bourbon cosponsored the tour with his publisher. We selected a collection of cocktails and recipes from the book for the set and Morgan did interviews with markets including Albuquerque, Atlanta, Bakersfield, Chattanooga, Greensboro, Kansas City, Las Vegas, Mobile, Phoenix, Roanoke, San Diego and St. Louis.

Murphy also did a sponsored radio tour by another bourbon company—Four Roses—and did 15 radio interviews. By working with sponsors, Murphy was able to extend the reach of his book campaign.

QVC (and occasionally HSN)

Television shopping channels have become fantastic selling opportunities for cookbooks. If you can get booked on David Venable's show, "In the Kitchen with David," which airs on Wednesdays at 8 p.m. and Sundays at noon, you have a chance to hit the *Publishers Weekly* bestseller list. QVC requires an exclusive, pre-on-sale window, which means, like online preorders, all of your sales are recorded on the first day on sale—sometimes as many as 10,000 copies! The secret to success is creating an incredible spread with a variety of dishes that you get David to eat. If he likes something, he does his "happy dance" and his fans go crazy and start shopping. Yes. It's that weird and that simple. It's not as simple though to get booked. The QVC buyers are quite a selective bunch. They know exactly what will work for their audience and what won't. If they select your book, you will be required to attend QVC school in West Chester, Pennsylvania in advance of your experience. This is a combination media training and audition. If you fail QVC school, and you can for a variety of reasons—poor television presence, inability to make message points, bad chemistry with the test host—your booking will be cancelled and you'll have lost your chance. Make sure you take the training extremely seriously. Read all of the materials in advance and go in ready to shine.

In this chapter, I've tried to condense 20 years of experience into 5,000 words. I admit that it is possible to achieve media attention without the guiding hand and expertise of a professional, but it's certainly not easy and requires an enormous investment of time. Truth be told, it's not easy and requires an enormous amount of time, *even for professionals*. It's a tough business. Professionals can get you in the door, but ultimately it will be up to you to deliver a good book, a great television appearance or an engaging interview.

Chapter 10

E-books and Innovation, Plus Just a Wee Primer on Self-Publishing

Have you heard the story? The one about how the book publishing industry is toast. No one wants to go to a bookstore anymore. You can get all the content you need for free online. No savvy person would actually still purchase a cookbook. The truth is, like every other media institution currently in existence, the book industry is embroiled in transformation. But the good news is cookbooks still sell. According to *Publishers Weekly*, nearly 25 percent of the nonfiction bestsellers in 2013 were about cooking and nutrition, which means cookbooks are the biggest success story in the nonfiction category (the rest of the winners in the field, by the way, were mostly about *Duck Dynasty*!).

People will never give up the tactile joy of holding a cookbook in their hands—and putting it to good use in their kitchen. But they also don't mind getting recipes in thousands of other ways as well. And that's why the new frontier of cookbook publishing could be an exciting place for you to be. Realistically, it might be your only option if traditional publishers just aren't biting. But you also might be one of those special souls who prefer to color outside the lines, see the world differently from everybody else and know exactly what's been missing in kitchens around the globe.

Plus, nontraditional mediums—developing a culinary app or self-publishing a hard copy or an e-book—can happen faster and appeal to a niche audience who so love what you have to say—and how you're saying it— they'll help you find even more fans. And just like social media, if you can show evidence of success, there's a good chance you will get picked up by a traditional publisher and get a second shot at a larger audience. Let's quickly consider the pros and cons of going this route.

PROS
- Complete editorial control.
- If done successfully, it can be a means to getting published by a larger company.
- It will be like a boot camp for learning ALL stages of publishing and that versatility can serve you well professionally in today's world.

CONS
- Because it will be boot camp, you will need to quickly learn about EVERY aspect of publishing instead of relying solely on the experts.
- No matter how much you learn, you will have to pay out of your own pocket to ensure the design, distribution and printing, etc. are up to par. The amount varies but typically can be thousands of dollars.
- Distributing your book will be incredibly difficult.
- Getting into bookstores will be incredibly difficult.

Just a reminder...I wanted to write this book to help people find success writing a cookbook in the traditional sense. If you are serious about self-publishing—digitally or print—you should read the multitude of books or online articles that go in-depth about the subject. There's an entire website devoted to the subject (selfpublishingadvice.org) and an expo (selfpubbookexpo.com) held every year. This chapter will offer some preliminary steps to get you started on that front. More importantly, I hope it may inspire you to think about developing a cutting-edge idea of your own in the next few years. This is a great time to make waves and try something completely different.

Spotlight:
Nick Fauchald and Short Stack Editions

One of my favorite pioneers in this new frontier I'll call cookbook 2.5 is Nick Fauchald. After 10 years in print media, he decided to go digital in 2008, launching the food site Tasting Table. But he still believed there could be something even better. "After a few years I had enough perspective on both sides of the fence to realize the two are not working well together a lot of the time," he explains. "Digital has the strength of speed, flexibility and innovation but its weaknesses are the old-fashioned things print did well like quality control, ethics and overall care. Digital needs to learn that bells and whistles alone don't make a successful product for long." His concept? Why not create products that truly bridge the strengths of digital and print

First, he cofounded Short Stack—a series of small-format, single-ingredient cookbooks inspired by recipe pamphlets that brands like Betty Crocker and Crisco used to put out 50 years ago. "I collected them and so did my mom," he recalls. "They are part of American food culture. I wanted to do a modern version." He reached out to three accomplished recipe developers and asked them to write 20-plus recipes on a subject of their choice. The result? *Strawberries* (by food stylist Susan Spungen), *Tomatoes* (by culinary consultant Soa Davies) and *Eggs* (by former *Gourmet* magazine editor Ian Knauer). By the way, Nick really wanted to make hard copies of the books, instead of digital ones for a reason. "We're trying to make a statement that physical cookbooks are so important and useful and will be around for a while." (Be still my heart! See why I love this guy?)

But wait, that's not all. There was an even bigger philosophy percolating in Nick's mind. "The idea was to do something physically on paper," he says, "and to harness all of the tools of the Internet and digital world to fund it, market it and sell it, to get the most successful print product we could."

(continued)

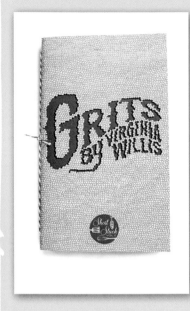

Short Stack's first move was to use the very modern phenomenon of crowdsourcing to finance their contemporary twist on a nostalgia product. With help from Kickstarter, they found 1,761 backers and raised $92,672 (the original goal was $50,000). Now there are 10 of these books available, with several more on the way—including ones about grits and buttermilk. Yum! You can buy them for $14 each, $38 for three or order a yearly subscription for $75. (Check them out at shortstackseditions.com.)

Nick also revolutionized how to pay his cookbook contributors. "It's a reverse of the traditional royalties model where you get a biannual check based on sales," he says. "We pay based on every time we print copies of the book. They don't have to worry about how it sells. They get paid no matter what."

I contend though that Nick's business plan actually encourages those authors to put good time and energy into helping promote their work. His marketing plan involves celebrating each edition with a very cool bookmaking event where readers can watch the authors' cooking demos and participate in craftsmanship that goes into making each stitch-bound book by hand—it's like a good old barn raising.

In addition to Short Stack, Nick is using his business plan to custom publish books for other chefs. He's currently updating old cookbooks from grand dames Serena Bass and Nancy Harmon Jenkins as e-books. "Reviving their work is an untapped market," he says. "They're good examples of how an e-book can really enhance the original." Nick and his team add updated recipes and photographs as well as a video component. It gives new life to old classics as well as allows chefs to showcase their storytelling chops.

SELF-PUBLISHING 101

If you are seriously considering self-publishing your cookbook, Terry Walters's story should give you some hope. She's been at the forefront of the clean eating movement ever since she was diagnosed with high cholesterol in college. After playing around with ways to make kale and brown rice taste better and attending the Institute for Integrative Nutrition in Manhattan, she became a holistic health counselor and teacher. Her clients urged her to compile her recipes in a book so she self-published *Clean Eating* in 2007. Mario Batali loved her recipes so much he called it "the most exciting book based on fresh produce and simple recipes I have used in years." That helped get her an agent and then Sterling Publishing came calling. Since being distributed by a traditional publisher, Walters has been nominated for a James Beard award and has become an in-demand public speaker.

I also adore the story of Bruce Cadle, the "date night chef." He self-published a book called *Party for Two*, inspired by the romantic dinners he and his wife Valerie enjoyed for over 30 years of marriage, and earned a space in the top 10 on Amazon's hot releases last year. Cadle told the Muy Bueno blog that he had no marketing budget so "I had to be really focused in order to make an impact. I built a Facebook friend base of over 4,000 people and held a Virtual Release Book Party. I got several really good advance reviews but didn't release them until the party. For one hour on the release day I hosted the virtual party with trivia questions and prizes. I asked everyone to share the link to *Party for Two* on their Facebook walls. The results amazed me. *Party for Two* made Amazon's bestseller list in the cooking category, its general Hot New Release list, and went on to number four in its Hot New Release cooking category."

Based on these anecdotes, it's not a huge surprise that the self-publishing industry is expanding. According to *Publishers Weekly*, self-published print books increased by nearly 30 percent in 2013 (interestingly, the rate of self-published e-books declined ever so slightly in 2013, down 1.6 percent). And if self-publishing is for you, you're in luck because the industry has become more sophisticated yet easier to navigate. The largest and best-known companies are CreateSpace (which is run by Amazon), Smashwords and Lulu. But according to Topconsumerreviews.com, Outskirt Press, Virtual Bookworm, Books Just Books, Iuniverse, Trafford Publishing and Lumina Press are also worth checking out. I urge you to shop smartly—read customer reviews!—because every company does not offer the exact same services and has different costs, fees and royalty plans. David Carnoy may not be a cookbook writer, but the tech expert has given lots of good advice online about the perks and pitfalls of self-publishing (something he knows about since the formerly self-published thriller writer now has a deal with an independent publishing company). One tip from him, in particular, resonated with me. When it comes to the creative part of making a book, deal with experienced creative folks, not just the staff at the company. "If you can, it's better to hire your own people and work directly with them," he has said. "Ideally, you should be able to meet with an editor, copy editor iand graphic designer in person—and they all should have experience in book publishing." Because as he also says in his column, "Self-publishers don't care if your book is successful. They say they care, but they really don't care. You have to make them care."

E-BOOK 101

Many people who self-publish decide to print a hard copy as well as a digital one. But for some, it's strictly online. And why not, since many e-books now have the ability to include exciting interactive features like embedded links, video narratives or even cooking demos (people in the publishing industry called these "enhanced" books). Still, the consensus seems to be that an e-book may be easier and cheaper to create but much harder to market. "Apple iBooks is a great piece of software that makes something very professional looking," says my guru, Nick Fauchald. "But even if you get Apple behind you it doesn't do that much for you in the end." A brief glance at the 20 top-selling digital cookbooks on iBooks offers perspective on the matter. More than half of the bestsellers fell into the special diet genre and less than a third came from a boutique publishing company. And only one author was self-published (more on her below!). The news was a little more optimistic on Amazon's list of bestselling e-cookbooks around the same time. Four out of the top 10 were from independent publishers—again, only one was actually self-published.

So how did Danielle Walker's e-book, *Thankful*, end up on the top-10 list of bestselling e-cookbooks near the end of 2014? The fact that "*New York Times* bestselling author" was already on her resume probably helped. Walker's story began when she was diagnosed with an autoimmune disease called ulcerative colitis. Like many others, she chronicled her attempts to switch to a different kind of diet on her blog *Against the Grain*. Eventually, she did a book on the subject that became a huge seller.

Just a year later, Walker followed up the print book with an e-book of 25 recipes for Thanksgiving. It's available for $1.99 on Amazon Kindle or Apple iBook or $4.99 as a PDF straight from her blog. She explained her reasoning in a post on her blog. "Thanksgiving cooking alone is a daunting task. Every person has preconceived notions on what Thanksgiving should taste like. When you add to that the need to create a Gluten-fee and Paleo friendly menu, it sometimes can be a monumental task. So I created a Thanksgiving e-book. The goal of this book was to remove the hurdles to creating not only the recipes, but also the entire coordinated meal. I've set up a full end-to-end recipe book that will cover everything from the turkey to drinks. Ideally, this makes your job that much easier and your holiday more enjoyable! As I want everyone to have the ability to eat healthy this holiday season, I've decided to charge a minimal amount for the e-book. The rationale in doing this is that I want you to have the ability to download the PDF, share with friends and even print the pages you need to cook." Remember Will Schwalbe's tip about solving a need? That's what Walker simply did here—stop people's panic about what to cook for all their family members on special diets—and it's the reason her very niche e-book is one of the very few e-books to make it to the bestseller list.

Cooking Paleo is also the secret to food blogger Melissa Joulwan's success as a Kindle e-book author. (As I write this, her first book, *Well Fed: Paleo Recipes for People who Love to Eat* is number four on the list even though it was published a few years ago!) Like many other success stories in this book, the Texas-based Joulwan began with a blog and a mission to get healthier. In 2009, Melissa switched to a Paleo diet and posted new recipes on her blog Clothes Make the Girl. She received such a positive response from her readers she decided to do a cookbook. As she explains in her blog, her dream team consisted of her husband, a designer, her parents, friends and her cat Smudge. They tested recipes over and over for six months. The entire project cost her about $6,000 and she says she broke even in about a day and a half. It certainly helped that Joulwan and her husband had professional experience in social media, web development, advertising, marketing and photography. She offered free PDF samples of a portion of her book to get attention.

One answer struck me from Joulwan's interview with Diane Jacob's blog Will Write for Food. She had already written a book—about her experience as a kick-ass Roller Derby girl in Texas—but decided to self-publish because she had been dissatisfied with the experience. "The marketing all felt really off to me. It got put into the sports section, and I felt like the publicist was not invested in promoting the book. I was really bummed by the whole experience." And her advice for people interested in self-publishing? "It's going to sound very groovy and Marin County but the number-one thing is to know why you want to do the book and let that guide all of your decisions."

Translation? Always trust your gut and be single-minded about the focus of your book.

Spotlight:
One Cookbook Author's E-book Experience

Nancy Baggett posted this article on Will Write for Food on February 25, 2014:

After writing 16 cookbooks for mainstream American cookbook publishers over nearly three decades (a few of which I actually worked on), I just copublished my first Kindle book. It's a 250-page coauthored work called *The 2 Day a Week Diet Cookbook,* with 75 recipes and 50 color photographs for $3.99.

What made this project different was that, from the beginning, my coauthor Ruth Glick and I planned to create a Kindle book. We never considered pitching it to publishers. Ruth had already written a number of Kindle books (mostly novels), and when she proposed that we collaborate, I promptly agreed.

In retrospect, I can see how this self-publishing process would be daunting for inexperienced authors. Going the indie Kindle route meant foregoing a publisher's hand-holding and the usual editorial, production and marketing assistance. Having written numerous cookbooks, we felt confident doing the recipe development, editing and proofreading, and even writing blurbs. The jobs that were less familiar, particularly book interior layout and cover design, were taxing. But years of being part of producing cookbooks gave us a good sense of how to proceed. The feeling of stretching and growing and doing something new was gratifying, too.

For three reasons, self-publishing made sense:

1. **We had a solid team to produce the book.** Not only did Ruth and I have lots of experience writing healthy and special diet cookbooks, Ruth's husband, a retired computer scientist, was on hand to do all the Kindle coding and formatting. To balance his technical contribution, I took the 50 color photos. I'd been honing my food photography skills for several years and was enthusiastic about showing off my work in a book. I was involved with layout in several of my cookbooks, so I took the lead in design. We found a cover layout we liked, then asked a a graphic designer Ruth knew to produce a cover along the same lines, using my photos. In the process I learned more about Photoshop and I think I can produce an even better cover in the future.

2. **We saved time.** Interest in the diet (which originated in Britain as the Fast Diet or 5-2 diet) was heating up in the U.S., so we wanted to get our book out promptly, ideally by January 3, 2014. We bypassed the long, often tortuous task of writing a proposal and finding a publisher, and proceeded directly to manuscript writing and production. Though our publication date slipped slightly, we published on January 11, still in time for the legions of repentant dieters seeking salvation at the start of the new year.

3. **We're sharing in a much larger percentage of the profits than what publishers offer**. I've long lamented that content producers are at the very bottom of the compensation chain. Too often writers' rewards come in the form of personal satisfaction only. So, the Kindle model providing a royalty rate of 70 percent on books sold in its store for $2.99 or more has undeniable appeal.

(continued)

4. Cost was minimal. As far as cost, we spent $800. The biggest expense was buying the EHSA nutrition software to produce the nutrition labels. It was $700. The original cover work cost $75, and the ISBN was $25. I'm not counting any food costs, as we ate everything we created. We need to sell 286 copies at $3.99 to make our money back. It seems likely that we'll do that within three or at most four months of publication. If we can generate more visibility, it could happen faster.

5. Promotion was a challenge! Promoting a Kindle title poses several unique challenges. Since there is no physical book to show and talk about on camera, drumming up television appearances is problematic. Radio producers and newspaper editors are also a hard sell, probably because they worry that not enough viewers have Kindles. So we went to chat rooms, special interest forums, personal and guest blog posts, Pinterest, Facebook, Twitter and other social media formats where Internet- and Kindle-savvy audiences congregate. The drawback to being totally involved up to the very moment of publication, though, was not having much time for promotion. Ideally, to generate launch buzz, we should have laid some groundwork in advance.

Would I consider doing more Kindle titles? Absolutely! Although virtual books are perceived as less prestigious than and inferior to "real" books (and of course some *are* crude and amateurish), digital cookbooks can be a better buy. Due to the exorbitant costs of color printing and quality paper stock, if Ruth and I had made a print edition of *The 2 Day a Week Diet Cookbook,* we would have had to settle for fewer photos, printed it in black-and-white, or priced copies at about $30 each. The Kindle format gave us the opportunity to include enticing photos of nearly all the recipes, add color throughout, serve up a substantial 250 pages, and still offer our book at an amazingly affordable price. What's not to like about that?

Spotlight:

Tips for E-book Formatting From Designer Derek Murphy [Posted on selfpublishingadvice.org (October 10, 2014)]

#1: E-books are supposed to be responsive and fluid.

You can't set up everything exactly, because readers need the ability to enlarge the text, change the font, widen the line height; plus the e-book will look different on every device and previewing tool. Rather than add a lot of style, you need to *remove* as much style as possible and make everything very simple. Don't set a font for the main body text, although you can usually get away with it for chapter headings. You can insert images for breaks or decoration but keep in mind HD devices have higher resolution and will make all the images look really small. (You should start with images that are 1440px wide and try to keep them under 127kb still.)

The most important thing is that the text works and is easy to read—so if you're trying to do anything too complicated, let it go. Simple is usually the solution. Look at any mainstream published e-book—they rarely have special fonts or images and are super minimal.

#2: Start with your Word file.

The easiest way to make an e-book is to start by setting up your Word file the right way. Use line indents, not tabs. Use the "heading1" style for all chapter titles, and check that a table of contents is being made automatically. Set a new paragraph style for non-indents on the first chapter. There's an in-depth guide to this here: www.diybookformats.com/ebooks.

If you've done it right you can use a simple online e-book conversion tool, or upload it straight to Kindle, or run it through Calibre, and everything should look just as you set it up in Word.

#3: Working with an epub file

If you're using Scrivener, you'll be able to export an epub file but won't be able to make changes easily—you'll have the same problem with Calibre or automatic converters. To make changes or fix typos you'll need to download Sigil. Sigil can be complex to learn, but if you already have an epub file and are just making fixes, it shouldn't be overwhelming. You can also use Sigil to add fonts or images, or edit the style sheet (for example if you want the indents to be a little larger, or the subtitles to have more space below them).

InDesign will export an epub with fonts, but you'll usually have to strip out at least the body font attributes (because you want each e-book device to be able to handle the body text, so your book doesn't look strange or different than every other book viewed on that device).

For something with a little less of a learning curve than Sigil, you can try Jutoh—it's paid software but most of the options are pretty easy to find, including embedding fonts.

(continued)

#4: Online tools

Since an e-book is mostly a collection of different chapters—each set up like a web page, there have been a bunch of new sites recently that let you add chapters in one by one, use a simple "What you see is what you get editor" and export everything directly. They work similar to Wattpad.

Some of the interesting ones are:

- backtypo.com
- pressbooks.com
- tablo.io

But some of these require monthly plans, or that you use them for distribution. There's also a WordPress plug in so you can just put your chapters into your WordPress blog and export them from there. I'm building my own, and it's pretty slick so far, but not quite ready for release.

#5: Fiverr.com

But really it's much easier to let someone else do it. E-book formatting often costs around $100, but you can get it done for $15 or so on Fiverr.com (although it's still worth learning Sigil for when you find those inevitable typos).

There's one final platform I'd like to mention: the mobile app. This hasn't been universally perfected yet. As Nick Fauchald repeatedly tells me "people only use their phones and tablets to play Candy Crush Saga." But one young woman Down Under is proving there's hope for the culinary app—and amazingly enough she's done it completely new school, finding a following on Facebook and Instagram.

Five years ago, Belle Gibson was diagnosed with terminal brain cancer at 20 and given three months to live. Instead, she started blogging about how she believed holistic medicine and healthy, nutritious eating was helping to prolong her life more than traditional medicine. Once her efforts received an outpouring of online devotion she decided to create the world's first health and wellness app, The Whole Pantry. On it, you can find recipes, shopping lists as well as other resources and advice about transforming your lifestyle. It was downloaded 200,000 times in the first month, according to the *Daily Mail*. Apple came calling a year later, asking if the app could be included in their new trailblazing project, Apple Watch. Gibson told the *Sydney Morning Herald* that the collaboration with tech giant Apple had been a "whirlwind. We're very emotional and proud about it." But because I'm all about the joy of writing a cookbook, I'm even more impressed that it's the first culinary app to become a cookbook. Penguin Australia published her cookbook in October 2014!

Create your whole life. Download The Whole Pantry App today.

HERE AT TWP WE BELIEVE IN LIVING YOUR WHOLE LIFE. SO WE CREATED THE WORLD'S FIRST HEALTH, WELLNESS AND LIFESTYLE APP WITH A VISION TO RESTORE THE BALANCE AND EMPOWER THE WHOLE PANTRY COMMUNITY TO LIVE THEIR WHOLE LIFE. THE WHOLE PANTRY IS THE NEW GO-TO PLACE, FILLED WITH A CONTINUALLY UPDATING LIBRARY OF RESOURCES, EMPOWERING INFORMATION, LIFESTYLE GUIDES AND SIMPLE, YET BEAUTIFUL NOURISHING RECIPES.

INSPIRING RECIPES

LIFESTYLE GUIDES & INSPIRATION

Gibson's story proves that there only needs to be one person in the mix to figure out how to break with convention and blaze a new path. Who knows? By the time you're reading this, there could be hundreds of other chefs helping to make culinary app magic happen in kitchens around the globe. The world is evolving so fast I may have to update some of the particulars in this chapter as soon as it's gone to final print. (Fingers crossed it involves way less formatting and an app that does the after-dinner cleanup!) The message stays the same though no matter how much time has gone by. Technology will keep changing but people's love of food and hunger for help feeding their loved ones is everlasting.

Note from the Author

⌒∞⌒

Dear Reader,

This book was not easy to write. Not because I didn't love the subject—I couldn't love the subject more, and I ended up buying hundreds of dollars' worth of new cookbooks that I kept getting lost in during the course of the writing. This book was hard to write because I couldn't find the time to do it properly. Something else in my life, mostly work, kept getting in the way, because it was more urgent than my looming book deadline. Only through the incredible patience, support and the occasional threat of my publisher did it get across the finish line. I tell you this because you too will struggle to write your book. Cookbooks are big projects with many moving parts. Recipe testing is not only critical—it takes an incredible amount of time. I know authors who have tested the same recipe literally 100 times. They have written entire chapters of tested recipes and scrapped them, because ultimately they didn't fit in the final product (Jamie Oliver even scrapped [okay, back-burnered and repurposed for other uses] an ENTIRE book of vegetable recipes because his publisher and broadcaster wanted to change their focus that year!). I know authors who have turned in their final work only to have it rejected by their publisher.

All this is to say that writing your cookbook won't be easy, and it can even be a bit lonely. So I want to leave you with a game plan for a successful writing experience. Now that you know what you need to do, here's a few tips on how to do it:

1. Set real (and realistic!) deadlines and stick to them. Producing one chapter a week is probably not realistic, but testing all of the carrot recipes probably is—unless of course you're writing an entire book on carrots. Break the schedule down into weeks and then days. For example, if every Monday you put your grocery order in, that gives you all day to read last week's work and refine the writing. Tuesday, Wednesday and Thursday can be for testing and Fridays are marketing days. Post pictures of your testing all week, but don't get sucked into the social media vortex. Keep working and give yourself Friday to engage with your world. If you have a big week of testing and lots of great dishes, host a dinner party on Saturday and get feedback. Be rigorous and strict with yourself. Don't let other commitments get in the way. The only thing that should throw off your schedule is an unexpected challenge in the process. Maybe one of your favorite recipes just isn't working. You've tested and retested and it still isn't right. Confusion and frustration set in and pretty soon your schedule seems impossible. What do you do?

2. ASK FOR HELP! Don't let one small (even if it feels HUGE) setback derail your writing. I know you have six more months, and so taking a few days off the schedule doesn't feel like a big deal, but believe me—an object in motion stays in motion, and an object at rest? An object at rest misses deadlines. Call your editor for a pep talk. Write a blog or Facebook post on your challenge and ask for suggestions. Invite a friend over for a tasting. Maybe you're being too hard on yourself. Send a piece of copy to a writer friend (everyone has a writer friend) to edit for you. Remind yourself that you are not alone in this and reach out for support.

3. Do the hardest things first. My first boss gave me that piece of advice, and as almost impossible as it is to follow, it's still the best. Whether big or small tasks, if you start procrastinating on the things you are dreading, you spend more time obsessing about what you're not doing, rather than just taking care of business.

4. Have fun with your work. Remember, you are the luckiest person in the world and living the dream. You are being paid to do what you love and should feel grateful and enjoy the process. If you're miserable while writing your book, you're probably writing the wrong book.

5. Once is never good enough. Every recipe, every sentence, every photo, needs to be scrutinized. Set the bar high. How can you make this sentence better? How is your book going to be the best—in every possible way? Test and retest. Write and rewrite. Shoot and reshoot. It will pay off in the end.

Good luck on your journey. You can find me on Instagram and Twitter @kimyorio and by email, kim@ycmedia.com. Ping me anytime. I hope this book inspires you to do great things, and I would be thrilled to be part of the journey with you.

Acknowledgments

Will Kiester and Marissa Giambelluca at Page Street...this one's for you. I can't thank you enough for bringing me the idea and then helping me turn it into a reality. Your encouragement, extensions and occasional angry letters were what got me to publication. The sail during my writing retreat remains a highlight of the summer of 2014.

I have to thank a few others too. Chrisi Colabella—my cheerleader—and Thomas Norton, my son, at the numerous times I veered off track, you two were there to remind me of my priorities and deadlines. Liza Hamm, taking my research and random thoughts and turning them into workable prose was a feat for which I will forever be grateful. I hope we can collaborate again very soon. Thank you to Paul Smetana for holding down the home front and Aimée Bianca for holding down the work front. You two made it possible for me to carve out the space to get this done. Thanks to my brilliant writer/sister Kara Yorio for always dropping her copy to read mine, even when she was up against her own deadlines. For all of my colleagues and friends in publishing—your contributions to these pages made the book something that I am proud to publish. And finally, I must thank Pam Krauss, because not only did she give me tireless counsel and interviews during the writing of this book, she gave me the gift of her daughter Phoebe Bradford, who has meticulously compiled every photo for this text as well as proofread the manuscript and the pages numerous times. Phoebe, you're the best new right hand I could have ever hoped for.

Thanks much to all. xxKY

About the Author

〜

KIMBERLY YORIO founded a boutique public relations agency, YC MEDIA (ycmedia.com) in 1998. The agency specializes in food and beverage and got its start in cookbooks. Kim has worked on hundreds of cookbook campaigns both as an in-house publicist and at her agency. She has coauthored four business books for women with her former business partner Caitlin Friedman, and considers cooking from books one of the great pleasures in life. She lives in Hoboken, N.J. with her son, boyfriend and his daughter. She spends most weekends hosting dinner parties and going to spinning class.

Index

◉

Note: Page numbers in italics indicate photographs.